HAUNTED
CEMETERIES
OF OHIO

HAUNTED
CEMETERIES
OF OHIO

E.R. CUTRIGHT

Haunted
America

Published by Haunted America
A Division of The History Press
Charleston, SC
www.historypress.com

First published 2022

Manufactured in the United States

ISBN 9781467151320

Library of Congress Control Number: 2022937941

CONTENTS

Contents

PREFACE

There are nearly fifteen thousand documented cemeteries in Ohio. Each of them holds fascinating stories, and many, at one time or another, have been considered the dwelling place of ghosts. In writing this volume, I have selected thirty of these places where the hauntings act as an extension of the epitaphs and connect the lives of the long dead to the present. Sometimes the history and legend meet. Other times they do not, and occasionally, that's where things get really interesting. These stories range from the well known to the obscure, and I hope that even the most ardent fans of the supernatural, Ohio history and cemeteries will find some merit in these pages.

For those who choose to investigate or explore any of the locations listed in this book, it is important to remember that cemeteries are places where we commit to the earth our most cherished and loved family and friends. While visiting such places, be respectful of the grounds and of those who may also be there for the purpose of mourning or remembrance. If you are visiting a private burial ground, permission from the property owner is required; if you are going to a public cemetery, always obey the rules and closing times. If there are no welcome hours posted, it should be assumed that the cemetery is closed from dusk 'til dawn.

Thank you for reading *Haunted Cemeteries of Ohio*.

ACKNOWLEDGEMENTS

This book would not have been possible without the help of an endlessly supportive community of family, friends and strangers. First and foremost, I am very grateful to The History Press acquisitions editor John Rodrigue for giving me this wonderful opportunity and being patient as I figured out what I was doing. The same goes for senior editor Ryan Finn and the rest of the staff at The History Press and Arcadia Publishing. Thank you all!

None of the stories would've been possible without the help from a whole host of libraries and librarians from across the state. From Laurie Miller with the Ohio Library Council, who serendipitously brought fifty librarians to me at the start of this project to Judy Deal who helped me nail down a last-minute citation: you are all invaluable treasures! The same is true of various historical societies, local historians and cemetery staff who have offered up their assistance: Elissa Leach, Carol LeMasters, Randy Rogers, Sabrina Schnarrenberg, Mike Clephane and countless others. I appreciate you endlessly!

I owe a huge debt of gratitude to my local creep scene for reasons too numerous to mention: the Gals in the Graveyard, Wendy Everett and Zabrena Zellers Stahl; Lesley Fogle and Constantine Hondroulis of After-Death Plan; Tiffany Boggins, Jason McFly Kincaid and the staff at Witchlab; Julie Macala, Ian Hopper and Roasted Thumb Productions; Melissa and Bob Ray Starker; Whalin' Rob and Regan Jones; Cody and Shandi Holland; Buster and Geoff of Team Mephis"toes"pheles; and Lori Gum and Shane

McClelland of *The Q Files* podcast, whose push to find the true story of Hester Foster was the impetus for this work.

Thanks to my wonderful network of friends: Geeta Dalal, A.H. Lauber, Matt Hass, E-mae Holmes, Cynthia Westover, Scott Orts, Amy Oswalt, Babs Eicke, Julie Kimmet, Chris Luzio, Jessica Koons, Aubrey Cenci Stevens, Scott Stevens, Keith Thompson, Brian Dunfee, Lara Ranallo, Fana Beyene, Mary Shumway, Jacob Shumway, Mike Gifford, Christine Rohweder, John Schumacher and one thousand others for your technical, psychological, emotional and hysterical support.

Thank you to my loving and patient mother, Mary Lou Dixon, and my family: Lynne, Rich, Chase, Kim, Taylor and Zac. Also, a very special thank-you to Sharon Farrar, Elra Farrar and Loren "Bud" Farrar, for giving me all the support in the world. I don't know what I would do without each of you in my life!

And thank you to Martin Brennan, for always putting the coffee on, dealing with the ghost that I became throughout the writing process and having faith in my vision.

INTRODUCTION

C arl Logies didn't believe in ghosts—that is, not until he saw one. It was the summer of 1922, and the Painesville farmer was conducting his nightly check of the livestock when he first caught a glimpse of the apparition. He described it as a sort of "white shadow" that slipped past the barn and across the field. When Logies bought the farm a year earlier, he had heard that it was haunted but chalked the stories up to superstitious neighbors. His skepticism faded, however, when he began to see the white shadow more and more frequently—always at the same time of night and always with it first appearing at the barn and then moving across the field.

Early on in these encounters, the bewildered man tried shooting the figure, and when that proved futile, he started following it, noting that it always disappeared in the vicinity of an old, unused well.[1] In time, he became convinced that the apparition was in some way connected with the spot, and that August, he set about removing the large rocks that a previous owner had used to fill in the watering hole. His hunch was proven correct when he got to a depth of twenty feet and found a deteriorated shoe filled with bones. The sheriff and coroner were called out, and further clearing away of the stone revealed the skeleton of a man who appeared to have been struck down by an axe.[2] A watch that had stopped at 9:35 was also found, which happened to correspond with the time of night when the "white wraith" would be seen moving toward the well.[3]

The bones were identified by the timepiece and dental fillings as those of Henry Lipinstock, a hired hand who had gone missing while working at the farm seven years earlier. That night and into the next day, Logies's dog howled and whined incessantly, only calming after the remains were conveyed to the local cemetery and given a proper burial. Frank Lerman, the man who owned the farm at the time of Lipinstock's disappearance, was charged with the murder and taken into custody, although he was ultimately freed the following April due to insufficient evidence.[4] Despite the lack of a conviction in the murder case, Lipinstock's ghost was never seen again following the interment of his remains at Evergreen Cemetery.[5]

This well-documented case from 1920s Northeastern Ohio is almost identical to an account from Athens, Greece, that was recorded by Pliny the Younger during the first century AD. In his letters, Pliny wrote about a philosopher who lived in a haunted house and was one night led to an unmarked grave by its ghost. After the bones were discovered, they were given a proper burial, and like the shade of Henry Lipinstock, the spirit was neither seen nor heard from again. Similar tales told throughout the course of human history hint at the possibility that after we die, some sentient part of us might still be entwined with our earthly remains and affected by their mistreatment. Even though the Buckeye State has only existed for a few hundred years, locally the belief in this link between ghosts and the grave is thought to date back nearly three millennia.

When the first non-indigenous people arrived in the territory now known as Ohio, they discovered a landscape strewn with more than ten thousand strange earthen structures. The native populations were asked about these mysterious embankments, but they claimed no knowledge of their purpose or origins. Some were large geometric shapes that lay in open plains, others followed the contours of hilltops like ancient fortifications and certain earthworks seemed to take on the shape of giant animals rising from the ground and stretching across the landscape. Most of these enigmatic formations, however, were rounded, cone-shaped mounds. These ranged from subtle rises in the earth to abrupt peaks towering nearly seventy feet in height. Upon investigation, it was discovered that many of these mounds contained human remains and grave goods. They were, in essence, mortuary structures, and most of Ohio, it appeared, had at one time been a graveyard.

Today, the construction of these earthen tombs is largely attributed to two ancient indigenous cultures: the Adena, who lived in the region between 800 BC to AD 1, and the Hopewell, who flourished here from AD 1 to AD 400. The archaeological record indicates that both cultures reserved mound burial for special individuals within their societies, such as healers or spiritual leaders who were thought to have the ability to transition between the worlds of the living, the dead and the purely spiritual. When these mystics died, they were placed in a grave along with the sacred tools they used to move between the realms. This would include objects like musical instruments, platform pipes or, in one instance, a fearsome bone mask stitched together from the fragments of a human skull.[6]

In the case of the Adena, once the funerary rituals were complete, they would mound over the grave, and when later spiritual leaders passed away, the process would be repeated on top of the burial, creating a sort of vertical cemetery. The death rituals of the Hopewell were a bit grislier. Typically, they would strip the dead of their flesh, cremate the remains in clay basins and then bury what was left in the floor of charnel houses. After a varying number of these burials were made, the structures would be destroyed or dismantled, and the sites would be mounded over. The general population of the Adena and Hopewell cultures are thought to have been treated much less ceremoniously and laid to rest in common burial pits.

Scholars have suggested that, like many traditional indigenous North American cultures, the Adena and Hopewell believed that after death, an individual's soul would split into halves. One aspect of the spirit would enter the underworld, or domain of the dead, and the other would remain with the corpse as a grave ghost. There it would linger and watch over the body until it returned to clay.[7] Beyond the cliché of the "cursed Indian burial ground," grave ghosts have been part of many cultures across the globe. In Sumerian writings from 3000 BC, they were called the *gidim*, in the Norse sagas they were *haugbúi* and in ancient China they were known as the *po*. These entities were believed to have the power to wreak havoc on those who disturbed their burial sites, no matter whether the desecration was for plunder, progress or preservation. In line with these beliefs, many of Ohio's prehistoric mounds have developed a reputation for being home to the spirits of those who were buried within. They are Ohio's very first haunted cemeteries, and it is with one of these magnificent structures that this journey begins.

PART I

SOUTHEASTERN OHIO

MOUND CEMETERY, MARIETTA

Ohio would have a lot more stories that start out with the phrase "There used to be a mound here" if it weren't for the pioneers' knack for burying their own dead alongside these ancient tombs. Throughout the state, you can find cemeteries where the first burials (though rarely marked) were made well over one thousand years before the headstones, fences and gates went up. Some of these mounds are small and hardly noticeable, while others have been made unrecognizable after being intruded upon by more recent burials. In a few instances, they are large and dominate the marble and granite grave markers that surround them. Of all these ancient turned modern burial sites, none is more imposing or well known than the grand Conus Mound at Marietta's Mound Cemetery.

When Marietta was established in 1788, the area was home to a large complex of both Hopewell and Adena earthworks that encompassed much of what is now its downtown. The city's founders recognized the historical significance of the ancient architecture and vowed to preserve a few of the more impressive features as parks. One of these was the Conus Mound, a large conical structure that perched loftily on a hilltop overlooking the settlement. In a move that would later seem quite fitting, it became the focal point of a park called "Marie Antoinette Square." However, there was a change of heart in 1793, when the village and park's namesake was beheaded

Mound Cemetery's gates, where mysterious figures are said to lurk. *Author photo*.

by the people of France, and in 1800, the public square was repurposed for use as a burial ground. One year later, Colonel Robert Taylor became what is often referred to as the cemetery's first interment, which is correct, unless you count the inhabitants of the Conus Mound.[8]

Prior to 1801, the burial of Marietta's dead took place at the nearby Fort Harmar Cemetery or, quite literally, various patches of grass around town.[9] In 1839, the village decided to dig up these random burials and move them to Mound Cemetery. Because of these efforts, it contains the most Revolutionary War officers of any burial grounds in the United States. This includes historic figures like General Ebenezer Sproat, Ohio's first "Buckeye" (as he was called by the local Native Americans), and Commodore Abraham Whipple, whose sacking of a British navy vessel in 1772 precipitated the Revolutionary War. As an interesting aside, Whipple was also a distant ancestor of the horror author H.P. Lovecraft and is mentioned in his works *The Case of Charles Dexter Ward* and *The Shunned House*.[10]

Another body moved to Mound Cemetery in 1839 belonged to Sally Dodge Cram Green, a member of a prominent Marietta family, who had been sent to the Ohio State Asylum in Columbus a year before.[11] Sadly, she died while institutionalized there, and her remains were buried in the pauper's section of a local cemetery. Her son was sent to collect the body for reburial at Marietta, but when he arrived in Columbus, he found the grave empty. Suspicion quickly fell on the Worthington Medical College, which had long been rumored to source its cadavers from the city's graveyards—a once necessary, though understandably vilified, step in the quest for medical knowledge.[12] A few days later, a mob of outraged citizens stormed the school. They destroyed the building and ran a doctor out of town but recovered three corpses in the process, including the remains of Sally Dodge Cram Green, a pawn in the struggle between science and convention that now rests peacefully at Mound Cemetery.[13]

Speaking of grave robbing, in *Haunted Marietta*, author Lynn Sturtevant tells a bizarre and frightening story that reputedly took place in the cemetery when it was little more than a decade old. In those early days of Ohio's settlement, not much was known about the mounds, and there was often wild speculation about their contents and the people who built them.[14] For example, there was a legend that Conus Mound held buried treasure and

Abraham Whipple's poetic grave marker. Aside from his many accolades, Whipple was also a character in *The Case of Charles Dexter Ward*, written by his distant relative H.P. Lovecraft. *Author photo.*

was guarded by a curse that prohibited any man from looting the grave. On a stormy summer night in 1814, a group of women, thinking that their gender would protect them from the spell, decided to take a crack at pilfering the mound's prizes. So, under cover of darkness, they snuck into the cemetery and began to dig. They had only been at their work a short while when they heard the distinctive *clink* of metal hitting metal. This was soon followed by a jangling of coins. The excited troupe dropped their tools and drove their hands into the soil when, suddenly, they were met with a roar of thunder and brilliant flash of lightning that illuminated the ancient monument. It was in that moment that the would-be grave robbers saw a horrible, goblin-like creature atop the mound, glaring as it pointed down at them. The terrified treasure hunters ran for their lives and were so shaken by the experience that, even in the light of day, they refused to enter the cemetery to reclaim their abandoned tools.[15]

While the story of the guardian goblin is entertaining, it was probably concocted to discourage anyone who had ideas about the earthwork from acting on their curiosity. The only person known to legitimately explore the mound was Dr. Manasseh Cutler, who conducted a brief survey of the earthwork in 1788.[16] He found a single adult skeleton and several flat stones that might have indicated cremation burials but then stopped the excavation for fear of destroying the structure's integrity. After this, he went on to found Ohio University, serve as a member of Congress and lead a long and full life, seemingly unaffected by any ancient curses. However, just because Cutler didn't face the wrath of Conus Mound, that isn't to say the structure is without supernatural charms.

It's been suggested that the Adena and Hopewell, like many historic native cultures, believed that spirits of the dead were unable to cross water.[17] This idea is supported by the moat-like ditches that often surround their ceremonial architecture. When filled, these features could have been used as "ghost barriers," meant to either contain or protect against the spirits.[18] The ditch that surrounds Conus Mound is a large one, currently measuring four feet deep and fifteen feet wide. If it was intended as a ghost barrier, the people who built it took extra caution to ensure that no spirits could get close to the mound—or, perhaps more importantly, that none could get out. The moat has not held water for most of the cemetery's history, however, which might be why so many peculiar things have been reported near the structure.

One example of this strangeness are the unexplained lights that have been appearing on and around Conus in recent years. Usually these take the form of bluish orbs, although in 2018 author Mason Winfield witnessed

Conus Mound's large ditch enclosure, which some scholars suggest was designed to protect against ghosts. *Author photo.*

a brief flash that he described as a "red glint" in the branches of a nearby tree.[19] Such anomalous lights are commonly reported at haunted cemeteries across Ohio and around the world. Science has attempted to explain the phenomenon of these "graveyard ghosts" as phosphorous gasses that are produced in the human intestine during decomposition. Once there is nothing left to contain them, these fumes seep up from the grave, where they ignite when they hit the air, producing an eerie glow.[20] The Conus Mound is estimated to be about two thousand years old, however, and any gasses that it contained should have passed into the atmosphere long ago. The phosphorescent theory also does not explain the less vaporous denizens of Mound Cemetery.

One night, a group of young people playing flashlight tag among the tombstones had an up-close encounter with someone they couldn't quite verify as "living." When they first noticed the man, he was at a distance, watching them from the cemetery gates. After being spotted, he slowly walked toward where they were gathered and then paused in front of a large marble marker that stood nearby. He was dressed in what they could only

The ancient Conus Mound stands thirty feet tall and is known to contain at least one burial. *Author photo.*

describe as an old military uniform, and his eyes had a dark, discomforting quality that made the group feel as if he were still focused on them, even though he had turned to face the grave stone. After a moment, he walked back to the cemetery entrance, where he again fixed his gaze on the young people. Uncertain what to make of the stranger, they shot one another nervous glances, and when they looked back at the gates, he was gone— although none of them saw him leave.[21] Neighbors have also reported mysterious soldiers in the cemetery at night,[22] and sightings of an ominous, hooded figure lurking around the entrance after dark have prompted calls to the police on several occasions.[23]

As frightening as experiences like this may be at the time, the people who are buried at Mound Cemetery fought to create a nation, forged a life out of the untamed wilderness and, in a few instances, presided over a mysterious yet fascinating culture during America's ancient past. Consequently, any visit to this burial ground should be made with the utmost respect, and if you happen to find yourself in the position to interact with one of the apparitions that reside here, consider it a privilege. Things don't always go so well for those who do neither when visiting haunted cemeteries.

The Athens Pentagram, Athens

After members of the Delta Tau Delta fraternity stole a tombstone from a cemetery with a notorious reputation, strange things started to happen around their Ohio University chapter house.[24] Lights would flicker on and off, doors opened and closed by themselves and a window inexplicably slammed shut so hard that it shattered. Residents found themselves unable to sleep at night, and some even claimed to have been injured as a result of the disturbances.[25] Suspecting that the stolen headstone was to blame, they returned it to the grave, and as quickly as it had begun, all the unusual activity in the house ceased.[26]

The tombstone came from Simms Cemetery, the primary feature of a long-standing legend in Ohio ghost lore known as the Athens Pentagram. True to its name, this legend concerns a series of burial grounds in the area surrounding Athens that allegedly form a five-pointed star when connected on a map. Depending on whom you talk to, this sigil, with its points marked by places of the dead, either acts as a protective seal or does just the opposite and invites the spirits to manifest and convene there. Exactly where "there" is, along with most of the cemeteries involved, is also a matter of debate. Some believe that the epicenter is on Peach Ridge, a sparsely populated area northeast of town, although many consider Ohio University's Wilson Hall to be the heart of the Pentagram. Others contend that there are cemeteries scattered all over the place and that it is just as easy to use them to draw a puppy or a pony as it is a pentagram. Either way, one thing most of the theories have in common is that Simms Cemetery is the northernmost point of the symbol.

Located on the wooded slopes of Peach Ridge, Simms Cemetery is said to be the old stomping grounds of a wicked judge who took great pleasure in personally carrying out the punishment of those he declared guilty. This usually resulted in them hanging from a large tree near the cemetery and then being buried beneath its sweeping branches in unmarked graves. For many years, there were claims that on certain nights these victims of backwoods justice could still be seen, their bodies swaying ever so slightly in the breeze as they dangled from the tree limbs like ghastly Christmas ornaments. Not only are those anonymous dead believed to haunt the cemetery, but the spectral form of Judge Simms himself is also rumored to appear there. He's often been described as a hooded figure that chases off any who dare trespass on his private place of reckoning. His angry spirit is only constrained by Mary Roberts, a witch who cursed the judge for his misdeeds and was buried near him to bind the hex for all eternity, or so the story goes.[27]

The cemetery takes its name from John Wesley Simms, a Virginia farmer who moved his family to Athens in December 1840.[28] He operated a farm stand and tannery business three miles north of town and, alongside his wife, Nancy Jane, raised ten children—several of whom enlisted with the Union army during the Civil War.[29] The only known burials at Simms Cemetery are John, his wife and her father, sister and niece. While it's not unheard of for someone to have strained relations with their in-laws, there is no indication that his wife's sister, Mary Roberts, had ever uttered a curse against him.[30] Nor is there evidence that John Simms acted as a judge at any point in his life, let alone hanged anyone.

There was a dark moment in Athens history twenty years after Simms's death, when a group of vigilantes broke into the county jail and lynched Christopher Davis on the old South Bridge. Davis was a young, mixed-race farmhand who was awaiting trial after a fifty-two-year-old white woman accused him of attacking her with an axe and "outraging her person."[31] The event was well documented at the time, and for years afterward, the noose was gruesomely displayed in the back room of a local drugstore.[32] Had Simms been stringing people up decades earlier at his farm on Peach Ridge, it isn't likely that he would've had to keep it a secret. Regardless, the story persists, seemingly evidenced by the rope burns that were clearly visible on the supposed hanging tree at the cemetery, although it has long since fallen.

Even if the legend about the judge, his victims and a witch are nothing more than campfire stories, that's not to say that dark things have never taken place at Simms or other cemeteries in relation to the Athens Pentagram. During the 1960s and '70s, it was a popular destination for college students and locals alike, although there were whispers that underage drinking and pot parties weren't the only nefarious activities going on at the lonely burial ground. Those rumors were confirmed a few days after Halloween 1970 when, aside from the discarded beer cans and cigarette butts that could normally be found littering the site, an open grave was discovered.[33] While it's unknown if an actual exhumation occurred, one must wonder if this ghoulish deed was related to other attempts at raising the dead happening in Athens cemeteries around that time.

In late October 1969, a group of seven university students intent on conjuring a spirit climbed over the locked gate of Hanning Cemetery, in the hills south of Athens. They were led by a practicing warlock who professed to be a direct descendant of Rebecca Nurse, one of the twenty people executed during the Salem Witch Trials of the 1690s.[34] Shortly before midnight, the amateur necromancers—armed with a candle, a willow branch and a

Near this location at Hanning Cemetery, a group of Ohio University students attempted to invoke a spirit in 1969. *Author photo.*

vial of human blood—gathered around the grave of a man who had died on a Halloween long past. There they drew a circle of protection around themselves, lit the candle and began to chant: "I call upon you now, Spirit, to show yourself before us, to come before us and speak as to what we should ask."[35] Following several repetitions of this incantation, the blood was poured out onto the grave and the ritual was declared complete.

Just then, a chill wind passed over the congregation, the candle flickered and blew out and then everything went still. Nervous eyes scanned the darkness for any sign of a manifestation, but after a long wait, it seemed that the invocation had been a bust. Partly relieved and partly disappointed, a few of the students headed back to the cemetery's entrance. There they found that the gate, which was undoubtedly secured with padlock and chain when they arrived, had been mysteriously unlocked and thrown wide open. After double checking to make sure no one else in their party had managed to unlatch the lock, they were left to wonder if their call to the spirits had, indeed, been answered.[36]

One year later, another group of students held a slightly tamer séance at the cemetery using a Ouija board and two black candles. While the planchette of the Ouija board remained motionless throughout the proceedings, the

Hanning Cemetery's entrance as it appears today. The gate that existed there in 1969 was chain link fencing attached to galvanized steel poles. *Author photo.*

wax from the candles dripped down to form a cryptic message: "DAVT4." This was interpreted as a communication from David Tishman, a fourth-year student at Ohio University who was killed in a car accident earlier that year.[37] As brief as this possible message from beyond the grave may have been, it cemented Tishman in Athens folklore, and even though he's not buried there, his name is still known among those seeking encounters with the supernatural at Hanning Cemetery. On a more chilling note, some of those who've gone looking for Tishman's ghost have come back with stories of a different specter—one they say wears a long, dark, robe and brings with it mournful cries of the dead.[38] This phantom is yet to be identified, although the list of characters who fit that description is relatively small.

Another place consistently associated with the Athens Pentagram is Haines Cemetery, located three and a half miles to the northwest of the town's center. There are eleven people buried in this small family plot, one of whom is thought to be a Civil War veteran who went insane, murdered his family and now guards over his grave site. Like at Simms Cemetery, history doesn't support the ghost story here. The remains of one Civil War veteran, John A. Haines, are buried in the cemetery, but he died long before his wife and was considered a respected citizen of Athens County.[39]

The grave site of Civil War veteran John A. Haines and his wife, Salina, who outlived her husband by nearly thirty years. *Author photo.*

Also like Simms, Haines Cemetery is on private property, and anyone wishing to visit or investigate either place must first get permission from their respective landowners.

Beyond urban legend, the stories that surround the Athens Pentagram illustrate how spiritual energy and intention are sometimes directed toward burial grounds in ways the average person would never consider. They also demonstrate how cemeteries might be haunted by more than the spirits of those who are buried within them. Aside from entities that are summoned by curious college students dabbling in the dark arts, there is no shortage of stories about people being chased from secluded burial sites by menacing hooded figures. Most of the time these are probably just gloomy, bored teenagers. However, the open grave found at Peach Ridge hints at the serious and disturbing activity that can sometimes occur in these otherwise peaceful places of the dead.

OTTERBEIN CHAPEL CEMETERY, SOMERSET

Ghost stories, by their very nature, can often be quite nebulous. With every telling the details shift, depending on the interest of the narrator and the audience. Consequently, researching such tales can feel like wrestling with phantoms themselves. You grasp at something solid, only to find thin air. Certain truths evaporate before your eyes, and others suddenly manifest where you least expect them. On rare occasions, however, there is tangible evidence that keeps a story bound to immutable fact, and neither time nor the vandal's hammer can erase it. Such is the case at Otterbein Chapel Cemetery, the final resting place for residents of a long-forgotten village called Tattletown. One of the tombstones there has quite a tale to tell.

The story begins in 1843. That's when a Tattletown farmer named James K. Henry found himself faced with a problem. He would soon be thirty years old and had yet to settle down and get married, as was customary in those days. James Henry's bachelorhood wasn't due to a lack of romantic prospects, however. In fact, there were two local women who caught his eye: Mary Angle and Rachel Hodge. His trouble was that he couldn't decide which one to pursue. Complicating matters further, all three were friends, and James Henry feared that choosing one love interest over the other might cause a rift in their good relations. So, to avoid any culpability, he thought it best to place the decision in the hands of his almighty God and wait for some sort of sign.

The verdict was rendered one night, as far as James Henry was concerned, when his horse led him without provocation to the house of Mary Angle. He proposed that very evening, she said yes and the couple were married on January 11, 1844.[40] Unfortunately, the divine union barely had a chance to reach a trot before tragedy struck. Just one month after their first and only wedding anniversary, Mary died giving birth to a stillborn son. According to

Otterbein Chapel and churchyard. *Author photo.*

the family history, in the wake of the devastating loss, Mary's parents asked James Henry to return her favorite horse, which they had given the couple as a wedding present.[41] He refused to do so, and tensions quickly arose between the widower and his in-laws.[42]

Following a respectable period of mourning, James Henry turned his attentions to Rachel Hodge, and the two began courting. This probably didn't do much to improve the Angles' regard for James Henry, although the most notable dissent of the relationship wasn't from the living, but rather from the grave. Unearthly moans were heard coming from the corner of the cemetery where Mary had been buried, and those who passed by at night claimed to see a weird glow hovering near her tombstone. Despite the reports of otherworldly protests, James Henry and Rachel Hodge were married at Otterbein Chapel on December 7, 1848.[43] By some accounts, the newlyweds even stood at Mary's grave following the ceremony.[44]

After the wedding, the strange occurrences at the cemetery intensified. What were once eerie glows now appeared as brilliant flashes of light that illuminated the countryside, and the faint moans were replaced with terrifying screams that echoed across the rolling fields. Most people who lived in Tattletown at this time avoided the haunted churchyard at all costs. One resident who didn't have that luxury, however, was the groundskeeper,

The fortified headstone of Mary Angle Henry. *Author photo.*

The mysterious horseshoe stain on the tombstone of Mary Angle Henry. *Author photo.*

and one morning he made a startling discovery while tending to the graves. It hadn't been there before—he was certain of that—but somehow, on the back of Mary Angle Henry's grave marker, the distinct imprint of a horseshoe had appeared.

When James and Rachel Henry were made aware of this new development, it unnerved the couple, but not enough to keep them from the business of being husband and wife. They went on to have four children together and were, by most accounts, happy.[45] All that would change, though, on August 8, 1859. That day started out like any other. Rachel made breakfast and woke the children, while James went to the barn to feed the horses. As she waited for his return, she noticed that it was taking him much longer than usual to complete his morning chores. Eventually, Rachel ventured out to the barn to see what was keeping her husband. As she walked through the doors, all the blood drained from her face and a scream rose from the depths of her soul. There, sprawled on the floor at the stall of his first wife's beloved horse, lay the lifeless body of James Henry. The clean imprint of a horseshoe marked his forehead from where the animal had kicked in his skull.

The horseshoe stain is still clearly visible on Mary Angle Henry's tombstone, and the story of how it relates to James Henry's death has been the source of cold chills and shudders since that fateful day. It even gained national attention in a 1928 article for the Associated Press.[46] In the mid-1960s, neighbors said that the spirit of Mary Angle Henry made itself heard once more, after vandals shattered her marker with a hammer. The stone was quickly pieced back together and placed in a protective fencing, after which the unearthly wailing ceased.[47] Since then, the ghost has continued to remain quiet, although a dim blue light is still occasionally seen hovering about the grave of Mary Angle Henry, and there are some who claim that they have heard the soft trot of a horse passing the graveyard in the autumn evening breeze.

SALEM CHURCH CEMETERY, WELLSTON

Nestled on the side of a narrow and winding road in northeast Jackson County, Salem Church Cemetery looks like an ordinary, even somewhat pleasant, country graveyard. The powder blue door and window coverings of the church give it a calm, gentle appearance, and the wooded burial grounds that surround the building recall the large, parklike cemeteries of the Victorian era. It's easy to picture children playing here after a summer service, a young couple taking an evening stroll or an elderly churchgoer pausing to reminisce at a grave of a loved one. While all these events have most certainly taken place in the graveyard's long history, the moments that live on in oral tradition at Salem Church are not the standard fare of a quaint, country chapel and burial grounds.

The original Salem Church was built in 1837,[48] after a circuit preacher by the name of Jacob DeLay began organizing religious gatherings for the local pioneers.[49] The first interment there most likely occurred in 1843,[50] although one legend tells of a witch who was killed and buried on the land long before the chapel and graveyard were established.[51] Her spirit is said to manifest as a shadowy form that is sometimes seen looming in the darkness, and in certain instances, she has even been said to scratch the arms and legs of unwary visitors.[52] It would be fair if one were to dismiss this as a campfire tale that makes use of the cemetery's shared name with Salem, Massachusetts, but there just might be more to the story.

A history of Jackson County from 1900 has several pages dedicated to the trouble witches caused early settlers there, as well as how their hexes would be combated through sympathetic magic.[53] If livestock were bewitched, either a portion of the animal's hair and blood would be burned, which was believed

A young woman's tombstone at Salem Church Cemetery. *Author photo.*

to bring injury back onto the person who cast the spell.[54] If the subject was human, however, even more drastic measures were taken. When one young Jackson County woman began having "fits" during religious gatherings, it was thought that she had been cursed by the wife of a local farmer. To defeat the witch, a profile of the accused was drawn on a piece of wood and then shot with a silver bullet.[55] This counter magic didn't kill the woman but supposedly made her so uncomfortable that she and her husband moved away.[56] Even though this is a far cry from murder, it demonstrates that early Ohioans were willing to harm those who they perceived as witches, and this particular ghost story might be closer to truth than we would think.

A more commonly sighted apparition at Salem Church Cemetery is the Union soldier who is often seen standing at attention beneath one of the graveyard's large cedars. This spirit has reputedly been guarding the grounds since the 1870s, and while its identity is unknown, the reason the soldier might haunt the place is less mysterious.[57] On July 17, 1863, Union forces clashed with an army of Confederate raiders at Berlin Crossroads, a small community just two miles west of the cemetery. The Union emerged unscathed, and the number of casualties on the Confederate side varies depending on the source, although it is generally thought to have been between four and twelve men. After the skirmish, Confederate general

The grave of a Civil War soldier at Salem Church Cemetery. The broken sword on the tombstone symbolizes a life cut short. *Author photo.*

The current Salem Presbyterian Church, which was built on the site of the original building in 1915. *Author photo.*

John Hunt Morgan used Salem Church as a temporary headquarters and place to bury his dead infantrymen.[58] So, perhaps it's the presence of these Confederate graves that binds the Union soldier to the cemetery, where he keeps his tireless vigil to ensure that these Southerners will never rise again.

The log structure used by Morgan and his raiders was eventually dismantled, and in 1915, the present building was erected on the site.[59] Due to a lack of membership, the chapel was closed in 1928 and sat unoccupied over the next twenty-two years.[60] Local folklore asserts that there was only one wedding in the church during those early days and that the bride died shortly thereafter.[61] On certain nights, it was said that her ghost could be seen moving from window to window as it glided down the aisle.[62] The building has since been shuttered, however, and this story, along with much of the church's history, has all but been forgotten. Yet there are some who say they have heard echoes of earlier times in the music and voices that sometimes drift into the cemetery from the vacant church, and it has long been said that if you knock on the chapel doors, *something* inside will knock back.

Mount Union–Pleasant Valley Cemetery, Chillicothe

Of all the haunted cemeteries in Ohio, there's a only a handful where the number of people who have claimed to experience the unknown aren't just in the dozens but the *hundreds*, if not greater. One of those places is Mount Union–Pleasant Valley Cemetery, or, as it is commonly called, "Elizabeth's Grave." This place checks all the boxes for a haunted cemetery. It's old, it's isolated and it is the setting of a tragic, though mostly unsubstantiated, legend. Sadly, it has also been almost entirely decimated by vandals.

The cemetery began as the burial grounds of Union Presbyterian Church, which was established on April 13, 1802.[63] Joseph McCoy, one of the organizers of the church, was the first to be buried there in the autumn of 1811, and over the next century, roughly two hundred people would join him beneath the soil.[64] Eventually, however, the church was abandoned, and the burial grounds fell into a state of neglect. In the years since, the lonely, overgrown cemetery has become a favorite spot for ghost hunters and adventure seekers who have reported a laundry list of paranormal activity. Batteries drain, devices malfunction and cars fail to start. Visitors hear disembodied voices that range from whispers to screams, are touched by invisible hands and encounter menacing shadow figures. People claim to have been chased out of the area by satanic cults, and occasionally, UFOs are witnessed in the skies above the old graveyard. Out of all the strangeness that goes on at the cemetery, though, it is most known for being haunted by a pale, spectral woman in a long, white gown whom the ghost lore names as Elizabeth.[65]

The story of Elizabeth and why she's thought to haunt Mount Union has several variations, although one detail most of them agree on is that she died by hanging from the branch of a large, foreboding oak tree that looms ominously at the back of the cemetery. In one telling of the story, a heartbroken Elizabeth, devastated by the death of her husband, took her own life there. In another version, men who wanted her husband's land murdered Elizabeth after his death and disguised their crime as a suicide. Whichever way she came to her end, generations of Chillicothe residents claim to have seen Elizabeth's ghost gliding across the cemetery or, most often, lurking about the tree where she reputedly died. The issue that has vexed paranormal researchers for the past several decades in relation to this haunting is that there are *fourteen* people named Elizabeth, or Elisabeth, buried at Mount Union Cemetery, and few records exist to determine which one might be the woman of legend.

Mount Union–Pleasant Valley Cemetery's headstones lie broken and gathered in piles across the fields. The tree on which Elizabeth was said to have been hanged can be seen in the distance. *Author photo.*

Part of the folklore surrounding Elizabeth's grave says that her tombstone moves from the front of the cemetery, where she is buried, to the back of the field beneath the tree where she died. Multiple attempts have supposedly been made to return the marker to its rightful place, yet it always finds its way back to the tree. The stone that has occupied that spot for the last several years belongs to Elizabeth W. Eagleson. The dates on her marker show that she died two years before her husband, which doesn't fit the legend, but it is from this tombstone that the mystery just might begin to unravel. Among a pile of discarded and broken headstones in the woods near the cemetery, there is a grave marker for Elizabeth W. Eagleson's sister-in-law, Elisabeth P. Eagleson. Aside from the possibility that these similar markers might have led to the rumor of a moving tombstone, aspects of Elisabeth P. Eagleson's life do match the legend. She died three years after her husband, and almost immediately after her death, there was a legal dispute over the ownership of the couple's 153-acre farm.[66] According to the historical record, no one killed her, nor did she die by suicide at the cemetery. She died in her home at the age of seventy-six from what the obituaries referred to as heart trouble and the Ross County death record lists as "old age."[67]

The tombstone of Elizabeth W. and William Eagleson, situated beneath a large branch of the infamous tree at the back of the cemetery. *Author photo.*

In some accounts, a woman named Elizabeth Augustus is said to be the source of the ghost story, but again, the circumstances of her life and death do not fit the legend.[68] She outlived her husband by nearly forty years and died at the age of ninety-six.[69] This discrepancy didn't stop someone from opening her grave, though, and until it was recently filled in, the large hole, which was usually obscured by weeds, posed a very real danger to cemetery visitors. Unfortunately, this level of vandalism has been going on at Mount Union since the mid-1980s, which might be part of the reason so many people have found it to be such an active location.[70] As mentioned earlier, history is filled with stories of spirits that have returned to the sphere of the living because they are angered by the desecration of their tombs. Given the scope of vandalism at Mount Union, which has only a few gravestones left intact, it's understandable then how the hauntings have branched out beyond the legend of Elizabeth, whoever she may have been.

WOODLAWN CEMETERY, IRONTON

Ohio was born at a time of great change. Not only was a young nation just taking shape, but the industrial age was on the horizon. One of the most prized materials during this period was iron ore, which was used to create machine tools, steam engines and a variety of other products that would fuel the advancement of manufacturing and distribution. As luck would have it, the iron deposits found in Southeastern Ohio were considered the finest in the country. Consequently, almost seventy iron furnaces were established there during the nineteenth century. The area flourished, fortunes were made and Ironton, which got its name because it was a place where iron was produced by the ton, became a boomtown.[71]

While the Industrial Revolution was taking place, there also was a shift in how we buried our dead. As more and more people were lured into the cities by factory jobs, the cramped living conditions led to an increase in the spread of disease. This, in turn, resulted in the overcrowding of urban cemeteries, which were viewed as unsanitary and thought to contribute to the problem by poisoning the wells. As a solution, many cities began establishing large cemeteries far removed from the population centers. The designs of these grounds were influenced by a growing appreciation for nature, the desire to escape the pollution created by industry and a more enlightened attitude toward death and mourning. The result of all these factors were the parklike cemeteries that can be found across the United States. This shift is most often referred to as the rural cemetery movement, and Ironton's answer to it is the fantastically storied Woodlawn Cemetery.

Established in 1871, Woodlawn was intended to be the finest place of repose for the town's citizens. On the day of its dedication, fifteen thousand people passed through Woodlawn's gates to the pomp and circumstance of the Union Coronet Brass Band and, undoubtedly, the demonstrations of several equally well-winded speakers. Despite the fanfare surrounding the cemetery's dedication, only six plots were purchased that day. It has taken nearly 150 years, but in the time since, approximately twenty-five thousand human remains have come to call Woodlawn Cemetery their forever home. Today, its current 100 acres are the final resting place of abolitionists, poets, riverboat captains and other notable people, like Nannie Kelly Wright, the only known female ironmaster and, at one point of her life, second-wealthiest woman on the planet.[72]

The sacred ground at Woodlawn also houses the ashen remains of the "Godfather of Goth," Edward Gorey. For those who are unfamiliar, Gorey was an author and illustrator most known for his dark, Victorian-themed works like *The Gashlycrumb Tinies*: an alphabet primer of childhood accidents, each with a humorous though fatal outcome. After his own death by heart attack in the spring of 2000, a certain portion of Gorey's cremains were mixed with those of his beloved cats and scattered along the beach and at his Cape Cod, Massachusetts home. However, the better part of the famous illustrator, author and playwright was quietly interred at the grave of his mother, Helen Garvey Gorey, in Woodlawn. Edward Gorey and his mother chose to be buried at this cemetery because, even though they never lived in Ohio, they considered Ironton their ancestral home.[73] While it might seem unusual that such a famously dreary character would be buried in an old river town cemetery without so much as a nod, it is worth noting that the remains of his great-great-grandmother Charlotte Saint-John lie just feet away, beneath an appropriately romantic marker. She was the namesake for his popular work *The Hapless Child*, which chronicles the tribulations of a young girl who is mistakenly thought orphaned, thrust into servitude and accidentally run down by her own father.[74]

Another moderately famous person with a much more visible grave site is Antoinette "Teenie" Sherpetoska Peters. Anything but hapless, as a child Sherpetoska was a dancer with the Russian Imperial Ballet and would often dance for Nicholas II, the last czar of the Russian empire. When she was a teenager, Sherpetoska immigrated to the United States with her family and settled in Chicago.[75] There she married James F. Peters, whose father founded Coal Grove, the Ironton suburb in which Woodlawn Cemetery is located and where she'd eventually be entombed. After their marriage, the beautiful ballerina toured the United States for several years, although the couple spent most of their lives in Chicago, where she operated a dance studio and he ran a steel company. Over the course of her career, she graced the cover of *Physical Couture* magazine and became a somewhat famous entertainer in USO shows during World War II. Overall, life had been very good to Teenie Sherpetoska. That is, until the night before her sixty-eighth birthday, when she was instantly killed in a head-on collision on Chicago's east side. Believe it or not, from there things would only get worse for the once-adored ballerina.

After her death, Sherpetoska was interred in a small but stately crypt at Woodlawn Cemetery. A short time later, ghouls broke into her vault and pulled her coffin onto the floor, shattering its glass top. Then they stole her most prized possession: a brooch given to her by the last czar of Russia. After that atrocity, they broke off two of her fingers while prying the rings from

The mysteriously refurbished porcelain portrait of Antoinette Sherpetoska Peters. *Author photo.*

her cold, dead hands. The indignities did not stop there. Mounted onto the side of the mausoleum were two porcelain portraits of Sherpetoska, one that portrayed her dancing and another that was a close-up of her at the height of her beauty. At some point, an unknown marksman took aim at the close-up, blasting two large chips from the image, and eventually, both portraits were stolen.

Despite her pictures being taken, not all visitors to Sherpetoska's crypt have missed out on her grace, balance and beauty. In the evening gloom, a glowing likeness of the ballerina has been seen performing pirouettes and pliés among the cold slab markers of her neighbors in death—seemingly impervious to the damage bestowed on her earthly remains. In keeping with this undying spirit, re-creations of her stolen portraits mysteriously appeared on the side of the tomb in the spring of 2021, although the whereabouts of the priceless jewelry remains unknown.[76]

As horrific as the mistreatment of Antionette Sherpetoska might have been, at least it occurred after her death. Sadly, the same cannot be said of Osa Drummond Wilson, who became a resident of Woodlawn Cemetery on February 25, 1911. The daughter of a farmer, she was only seventeen years old when she was wed to Scott William Wilson, a real estate manager who was four years her senior.[77] Osa's husband made good money and the couple would have six children over the course of their lives together, but the union was not a happy one.[78]

Rumor had it that during her pregnancy with their seventh child, Wilson came home drunk, started a fight and struck Osa so forcefully that she fell, heeled boot over petticoat, to the bottom of the stairs. The unborn child perished in the fall, and the mother followed a few days later. Her death was blamed on a short-term illness, however, and Wilson managed to evade a murder charge. To assuage his guilt, he had a beautiful monument to his wife erected over her grave. The years since have taken their toll, and the statue of Osa has lost both of her hands; those who give extra attention to the sculpture, however, have noticed an unusual discoloration on its right cheek that resembles a red handprint, earning her the nickname of "the slapped lady." According to cemetery lore, her husband had the statue repeatedly sandblasted during his life, but all efforts to remove the mark were unsuccessful.[79] Even sadder aspects of this haunted monument are the warmth and faint heartbeat said to emanate from Osa's slightly swelled stomach, as well as the very real tears that can sometimes be seen streaming down her granite cheeks.[80]

Yet another horrific tale of Woodland Cemetery concerns Dr. Joseph Lowry, a prominent Ironton politician and physician who, like Scott Wilson,

Osa Drummond Wilson's haunting statue and gravestone. *Author photo.*

spared no expense after the death of his wife. When Sarah Lowry passed away in the spring of 1931, Dr. Lowry had an extravagant, specially designed casket made for her, and because she didn't want to be buried, he also ordered the construction of a large above-ground mausoleum.[81] Once Sarah's coffin arrived, however, Dr. Lowry noticed that it was slightly scuffed and refused to settle for the damaged mortuary goods. Instead, he opted for a much less costly model from the funeral home's showroom and left the undertaker, J.S. Schneider, stuck holding the bill for the expensive, though useless, custom casket. The mortician would brood over the coffin and financial loss quite often.[82] Eventually, though, the worm would turn in his favor.

Two years later, Dr. Lowry himself was found dead. He was lying in his bed with his arms folded across the chest and a towel covering his face. The coroner discovered a bruise behind the left ear, his throat was discolored and swollen and blood from his nose and mouth stained the bed clothes.[83] There was conjecture that he'd suffered a stroke, although the talk around town was that the doctor had been done in by one of his political enemies or possibly even his heirs. Before the cause of death could be determined, however, relatives hired the funeral home of J.S. Schneider to prepare the body. When the begrudged undertaker saw who was on his table, the made-to-order coffin was pulled out of storage, and he then endeavored to fit the large frame of Lowry into the box that was originally meant for his much smaller wife. This not only involved cutting down the length of the doctor's legs but also slimming his midsection by pulling out the internal organs and restuffing the corpse with sawdust.[84] It was the perfect revenge, and he would've gotten away with it were it not for the suspicious circumstances surrounding Lowry's demise.

Several days after the funeral, persistent rumors of murder led to a postmortem examination of the doctor's remains. The investigation took an unexpected turn when wood shavings were found in place of lungs and intestines. Suddenly the undertaker had a lot of explaining to do. Under interrogation, he confessed to replacing the doctor's insides with sawdust and told the police that doing so was necessary for preservation purposes.[85] The excuse worked, and he avoided charges. Consequently, so did anyone who may have been responsible for Dr. Lowry's death. By the time Schneider led the authorities to the corner of his yard where he had buried the discarded organs, they were too decomposed to reveal any possible toxins, and the murder probe was dropped a short time later.

Dr. Lowry's ghost appears to get around quite well despite the undertaker having shortened his legs. He is seen wandering Briggs Lawrence County

The crypt of Dr. Joseph Lowry and his wife, Sarah Lowry. *Author photo.*

Library, the site of his former home, presumably looking for his missing innards. He is also said to haunt Woodlawn Cemetery, where he seems to be undaunted by his mangled corpse lying in a cramped and scuffed coffin. There he is reported to leisurely stroll the grounds arm in arm with his mother, Mary Lowry. The two are usually spotted near the entrance, although they always vanish before reaching the bridge that leads out of the cemetery.[86]

While manifestations of Teenie Sherpetoska, Osa Wilson or Joseph and Sarah Lowry are never guaranteed, no visitor to Woodlawn will miss seeing the enormous stone crucifix that dominates the center of the cemetery. Known as the Means Cross, this imposing monument marks the grave site of former Cincinnati mayor William Means and his wife, Martha Campbell Means. During its installation, a terrible accident occurred, and the stone toppled, crushing one of the workers. His spirit is said to lurk at the spot and, in one instance, scared a man passing through the cemetery so badly that he shot at the apparition, leaving bullet marks in both the cross and another nearby monument.[87] This leaves the question of whether a similar sighting is behind the rounds that were leveled at Teenie Sherpetoska's original portrait, and if so, did they do any good against fending off the ghosts?

Means Cross, the marker of William and Martha Campbell Means. *Author photo.*

One area of Woodlawn where the spirits would be more experienced with gunfire is the Civil War section. However, the horse-drawn hearse that is said to appear there in the early morning mist usually takes a backseat to the cemetery's more famous hauntings, and fortunately, there is no record of it having been fired upon.[88] It's uncertain which of the fifty souls buried at the veterans' field might bring about the manifestation of this old funeral coach. Perhaps it conveys a lost soldier who was buried in an unmarked grave on some Southern battlefield, bringing him home so that he can be reunited with his fellow servicemen on Northern soil. Maybe it's the last vestiges of some solemn moment where a family lost their only child to war. Or could it be Death itself, relishing in the great harvest it has reaped and then sown at the beautiful grounds of Woodlawn Cemetery?

PART II
SOUTHWESTERN OHIO

SMYRNA CEMETERY, FELICITY

Ohio's only witchcraft trial, according to most sources, took place in 1805 at the village of Bethel, just east of Cincinnati in Clermont County. The circumstances that surrounded this historic novelty involved two young women of the Hildebrand family who were suffering fits and hallucinations. Eventually, the young women became convinced that their elderly neighbor, Nancy Evans, had cursed them.[89] After various folk remedies failed to remove their bewitchment, the Hildebrands requested that a justice of the peace intervene, and a trial was set into motion. The best way to assess the soul of old Nancy Evans, the justice determined, was to weigh her against the Holy Writ.[90] To do this, a large wooden scale was constructed, and the accused was instructed to sit on one pan, while a Bible was placed on the other. If the book outweighed the woman, it was thought, then she was surely guilty of witchery. Fortunately for Nancy Evans, physics prevailed, and she was exonerated of all charges after sinking to the ground and sending the bible flying upward.[91]

Although it is less known, nineteen years earlier another woman had been accused of witchcraft just a few miles away. However, that was before Ohio had become a state, and in that instance, the outcome was much less pleasant. The story was recorded by John O'Bannon, a surveyor who was sent to plat out the section of wilderness that would become Clermont

County for the Virginia military in 1787.[92] On Christmas Day of that year, he was taking measurements in an area near present-day Felicity when his Native American guide shared a tale that touched his heart.

One year earlier, the guide told O'Bannon, a beautiful Shawnee woman by the name of Sweet Lips had been accused by her own tribe of sorcery and witchcraft. It was alleged that her spells had resulted in several failed hunting expeditions and lost battles. However, the true reason for the charge, said the guide, was that Sweet Lips had fallen in love with a white man named Hastings, whom the Shawnees had taken prisoner.[93] Her feelings for him were so strong that she betrayed her people by helping him escape and even promised him land should he later return to her. When this treason was discovered, it was decided that her dark magic was the cause of all the tribe's misfortunes, and she was sentenced to death. On the day of her execution, Sweet Lips calmly walked to her grave, knelt at its edge and prayed. As she did so, the chief stood behind her, raised his tomahawk and delivered a fatal blow to the back of her skull. The Shawnee women who filled in the grave said that, even in death, she maintained the beautiful smile that had earned her the name Sweet Lips.[94]

John O'Bannon was so greatly moved by this story that he recorded it in his field notes and implored the guide to show him the exact location where she had been buried, which he then marked with a stone.[95] In 1808, John Rankin, the famed abolitionist whose efforts Harriet Beecher Stowe immortalized in her book *Uncle Tom's Cabin*, built the Smyrna Presbyterian Church on the site, and a graveyard soon followed.[96] Today, only the graves and their markers remain at what is now known as Smyrna Cemetery, and although a man by the name of Hastings did move to the area a few years after her execution, the spirit of Sweet Lips is not said to rest in peace there.[97]

On dark, moonlit nights, people have claimed to see a young woman in the graveyard mist, bent down on her knees crying out for forgiveness.[98] What's so compelling about these sightings is that while the story of Sweet Lips is no secret, it's not widely known that she died kneeling at her own grave. Nor do many know that the rock believed to mark the true location of her death and burial still lies hidden within the boundaries of the cemetery. Yet not long before this book was written, a caretaker at Smyrna was summoned to that exact spot by a visitor who claimed to sense a tragic sadness there that predated the settlement of Ohio.[99]

Some have said that Sweet Lips's grave is marked with a stone that bears the ominous inscription "beware of her."[100] There is a very old, barely legible and crudely etched headstone that looks like it says something in this vein,

This cemetery sign at Smyrna is one of the only in the state to reference a burial that predates the settlement of Ohio. *Author photo.*

A recent marker created by preservationists for an unknown burial at Smyrna Cemetery. The obelisk in the distance allegedly glows at night. *Author photo.*

Headstone of Agnes Cooper, which has long been thought to read "Beware of her." *Author photo.*

but the name on the marker is Agnes Cooper. There is no definitive record of who Agnes Cooper was or why she would pose a threat to the living, even in death.[101] However, a close examination of photos taken by the Clermont County Genealogical Society in 2007 reveals a possible explanation. What appears today as a warning is most likely a misspelled and partially worn away epitaph that originally read "Agnes Cooper departed this world in the [illegible] year[e] of her life"—a common phrasing on tombstones during the early 1800s.[102]

Another location suspected of being Sweet Lips's grave site is a large obelisk toward the center of the cemetery that is said to glow on certain nights.[103] The monument is for Jane Woods, who died giving birth to her daughter, Leo Janette, in 1843. The inscription on the face of the marker says that they are both interred beneath the stone in a single vault. As for the light emitted by the obelisk, glowing tombstones are a common feature of cemetery lore, and there are quite a few others in Ohio that make the same claim. Most of the time, this phenomenon can be traced to natural causes, like the mineral composition of the stone or a particularly reflective polish.[104] Still, some say that they get an uneasy feeling near the monument, and during one investigation at the cemetery, a group of ghost hunters claimed to have seen a white, misty figure move behind the obelisk and then vanish.[105] For what it's worth, Jane and Leo Janette Woods died a week before Halloween, which is a time when many visit the cemetery in search of spirits. Maybe since it was near the anniversary of their deaths, they just happened to be visiting as well.

Darby-Lee Cemetery, Cincinnati

In 1890, a newspaper in Cincinnati ran a fantastical story about Noah Badgely, an early settler to the area whose prowess over the fiddle was said to be unmatched by anyone in the whole of the Ohio Territory. The article related how his playing could charm the birds from the sky, transfix and subdue would-be attackers and fracture crockery and glassware with its intensity. Through this exceptional talent, Badgely was able to earn a decent enough living that he never had to till his land, and it grew into a beautiful, grassy pasture known as the Fiddler's Green. There he vowed that his harmonies would continue to drift in the air long after he had gone. Delving further into the supernatural, he would go on to attest that, beyond pitchers or plates, his music also had the ability to "shatter the invisible wall which separates ghosts from living beings and loosen the sleeping dead from the imprisonment of the grave."[106]

This claim was put to the test one summer night when a native warrior visited the settler's cabin and implored that he use his instrument to call forth the spirit of Tenskwatawa the Prophet, a powerful mystic and brother to the famed Shawnee leader Tecumseh. The warrior told Badgely that Tenskwatawa had been killed in a battle between the Shawnees and Iroquois several years before and buried in a nearby ravine. The pioneer agreed to the request and, stepping out into the darkness, began to play a strange and eerie melody that seemed to resonate not just from the strings of his fiddle, but from the surrounding hillsides and forest. The low echoes from the landscape slowly built on top of one another, growing louder and louder until they created a deafening roar. The fiddle screamed above the din as Badgely trembled and swayed with the sawing of his bow. Just as the music reached a fever pitch, an arc of lightning tore across the sky, revealing a tremendous, ghostly sycamore tree and the dark silhouette of a person standing beneath its branches. In the wake of this spectacular flash of light, both the mysterious figure and the sycamore tree vanished, and so did Noah Badgely. A few days later, his cabin was found burned to the ground, and although he was never seen again, his enchanting music can still be heard between the rustle of leaves and in the soft evening breeze at Fiddler's Green.[107]

This story, which was written by the son of a well-respected Hamilton County land surveyor and presented as local legend, is a curious mix of fact and fiction. Noah Badgely was one of the original thirty settlers to what is now Cincinnati, having arrived on December 28, 1788.[108] However, he drowned shortly afterward while on a supply run to Kentucky.[109] Conversely, Tenskwatawa was not killed in a battle near Cincinnati, but rather lived to the age of sixty before dying on a reservation in Kansas. An editorial note at the end of the article gives the location of these events as a farm in Newtown, east of Cincinnati, although the ghostly portion of the tale was most likely inspired by accounts that have circulated for decades around an old family burial ground on Bender Mountain, west of downtown.[110] Some know this place as Fiddler's Green thanks to a 1963 play that heavily drew from the old newspaper story, although it's most commonly referred to as Darby-Lee Cemetery.[111] Today, this little patch of grass, which overlooks the Ohio River into Kentucky, is hidden in the woods behind the maintenance shed of a nursing home. At the back of the building, a path leads to a fenced-in knoll containing only a handful of tombstones and fewer than twenty graves. Several of them belong to the family of Revolutionary War veteran Peter Lee, although the majority are for members of the Darby family.

Henry and Margaret Darby were farmers from Virginia who moved to the Cincinnati area in 1818 and built a large stone house near the Ohio River. To supplement their income from farming, the house served as a wayside inn for travelers between North Bend and Cincinnati. It was also rumored to be a part of the Underground Railroad, operating right under the nose of frequent guests like William Henry Harrison, who, aside from becoming the ninth president of the United States, was also a slaveholder.[112] Legend says that Henry Darby would signal when it was safe for freedom seekers to cross the river from Kentucky into Ohio by playing his fiddle at the hillside cemetery and flashing a green-tinted lantern toward the south.[113] The strange lights and music earned the burial ground a haunted reputation among locals, which was likely encouraged by Darby. Even though Ohio was a free state, aiding in the escape of enslaved individuals carried heavy penalties prior to the Civil War. So, if his method of signaling escapees kept others from venturing too close and discovering his secret, it would've been all the better.

Darby-Lee Cemetery in Delhi Township. *Author photo.*

The marker of Henry Darby, whose spirit is still said to fiddle around the cemetery. *Author photo.*

Henry Darby died at the age of seventy in 1852 and was buried on the hill where he reputedly spent his nights using a lantern and music to usher people to freedom. The weird lights and sound of a fiddle being played at the cemetery did not cease with his passing, however. Could this have been the work of a family member who picked up the torch after Darby's death? Or maybe it was local memory that fueled the claims? One point against both these theories is that the unusual phenomenon is still said to occur there. Not only have ghost hunters seen a dim green glow moving through the trees or heard a fiddle playing faintly in the distance, but nursing home staff who were previously unaware of the area's history have also noticed the odd sights and sounds in the adjacent woods.[114] Henry Darby went to his grave never having known a United States without slavery, and there are many who believe the strange occurrences on Bender Mountain are the work of his spirit carrying on its noble task.

CLIFTON–UNION CEMETERY, CLIFTON

At the western edge of the historic village of Clifton, the Little Miami River takes a sudden and dramatic plunge. For two miles, the river dives and twists its way through a deep canyon of limestone and dolomite bedrock that was carved by glacial meltwaters some fifteen thousand years ago. Designated a national natural landmark in 1967, the cliffs at the gorge reach heights of eighty feet, and the scenic landscape draws throngs of nature lovers and hikers from across the state. Most are unaware that from this dark crevasse, many legends have clambered their way to the surface. Early accounts speak of daring escapes, tragic love stories and ancient treasure hidden within its depths.[115] There are also tales of ghosts.

During the early days of western expansion, pioneers took advantage of the turbulent waters of the gorge and constructed several mills there. This, along with its location along the trail between Springfield and Xenia, poised the area for development, and in 1811, the Clifton Presbyterian Church was constructed atop a hill just north of the gorge. Around 1813, people began to be buried in the churchyard, and although the building no longer stands, the old graveyard continues to be used under its current name, Clifton-Union Cemetery.[116] There lie the remains of a Seneca princess's daughter, victims from a cholera outbreak and one unfortunate soul known only as the "haunted burial."[117] The latter came about around

Clifton-Union Cemetery, where an unquiet burial allegedly took place around 1885. *Author photo.*

1885, when dreadful noises rose from the coffin during a graveside service. The sounds frightened the mourners so badly that, instead of checking to see if the person was still alive, they quickly filled in the grave and fled from the cemetery.[118]

Another area ghost story that has been passed along over the years involves a popular stagecoach driver who was found dead one morning, crushed by his overturned carriage near the cemetery gates. According to the legend, there had been a terrific storm the night before, and it was presumed that he had been racing to beat the rain when he took a turn too fast and met his terrible end. Because he was held in such high regard, people came from miles around to attend the funeral of the ill-fated man, who was buried under an old oak tree on the hill near where he died. That night and in the days that followed, the people of Clifton began to suddenly take ill, and many joined the stagecoach driver in the cemetery on the hill. The first to go were the men who had retrieved the corpse from the scene of the accident. It would soon become apparent that the driver had *not* been racing to beat the storm that fateful night, but instead was rushing to warn the village of a cholera outbreak in a nearby town—unaware that he had become infected as well. As a result, many of the people in Clifton died, and it is said that to this day a rush of wind can be felt, and a phantom carriage can be heard as it races along forever doomed to repeat its ill-fated final run.[119]

While this ghost story might seem too finely crafted to possibly be true, a curious gravestone at Clifton-Union Cemetery does, to a certain extent, support the tale. In an old section of the cemetery, shaded by trees, stands an unusually distinctive marker that towers over the surrounding monuments. Close inspection of its face reveals a harrowing stagecoach scene etched into the stone. A carriage led by four horses, which are depicted in full gallop, races through a copse of weeping willows. The coach wheels have circular lines, further suggesting motion, and a cloud of dust trails at the back of the ride. The profile of a single female passenger is at the carriage window, and the horses' necks are arched back with the reins pulled taut to the operator's footrest, indicative that the driver had lost control. However, the most haunting detail of all is that despite the position of the reins, the stagecoach has no driver. Beneath this engraving the stone reads, "Erected in memory of Lodrick Austin who departed this life September 1st, 1836. Aged 26 years, 7 months and 1 day." So, could this be the grave of the stagecoach ghost of Clifton?

In his 1932 book, *The History of Glen Helen*, W.A. Galloway wrote that Lodrick Austin was an expert young "whip," or driver, for a stagecoach line that carried guests to and from the water cure spas at nearby Yellow Springs. One night, Austin's horses became frightened by something and bolted while passing Clifton Cemetery. As the coach careened out of control, Austin was thrown from his seat and fatally injured when he struck a boulder by the cemetery gates.[120] No mention is made of the female passenger depicted on his gravestone, although the story otherwise fits with the elaborate engraving. While this is the generally accepted version of Lodrick Austin's death, it isn't the only one. A Clifton resident whom Galloway asked to explain the unusual stone early in his research told him that the young man had died of diphtheria a few days after dining at the local drinking establishment.[121] Another early resident of Clifton claimed that Austin fell ill with typhoid fever while driving through town and that, because he was too sick to go on, a different driver had to be found for the coach. Austin died there a few days later, and out of the kindness of their hearts, the people of Clifton had a beautiful headstone carved in his memory.[122]

While all three of these accounts share a thread with the ghost story, none mentions the devastating cholera outbreak that gives the tale its twist ending. The dreaded disease did, in fact, come to the village at the beginning of September 1849. The agent of death at that time was believed to be a

A close-up of the dramatic etching of Lodrick Austin's tombstone. Where is the driver, who is the passenger and what is the rush? *Author photo.*

stranger who took ill during an overnight stay at the tavern.[123] The next morning, the traveler died, but not before infecting seven other people there and another two who lived directly across from the establishment. Within a week, twenty-one deaths had occurred, and all in all, the disease took forty lives in the village.[124] Local tradition holds that these people were buried in a mass grave near the stagecoach driver in Clifton Cemetery, although some historians maintain that the low spot thought to be that grave is merely the site of the old church. Either way, the date of the outbreak absolves him from involvement in their deaths, even though the two events seem to have become tangled in legend.[125]

It will never be known why the young whip ran his carriage so hard that night in September 1836, what led the village of Clifton to give him such an elaborate memorial or who the lone passenger depicted on his tombstone was supposed to represent. Just as much as a phantom wind or the sound of wooden wheels rolling across a vacant gravel lane, these enigmatic questions ensure that the memory of Lodrick Austin continues to ride on.

Rose Hill Cemetery, Mason

At 4:30 a.m. on Friday, April 12, 1901, farmer John McClung left his bed, got dressed and headed for the barn to tend to his livestock. After feeding the horse and milking the cow, the seventy-four-year-old man returned to his home and climbed the stairs to wake his wife, Rebecca. When he stepped into the bedroom, he found her lying face-down on the mattress, the sheets and pillows surrounding her head stained a deep, crimson red. The old man alerted the other tenants of the house, who, in turn, summoned the village doctor. The physician's examination revealed that the woman had not suffered from some form of hemorrhage, as originally thought, but rather that her entire skull had been beaten so severely that every bone except for her jaw was shattered.[126] There would be no rousing Rebecca McClung that morning.

During the coroner's investigation, two pieces of tree bark were found near the body of the sixty-one-year-old woman, and it was theorized that firewood had been used to bring about her demise. It was common knowledge that the couple were wealthy, so initially, robbery was suspected as the murderer's motive. Yet it appeared that, aside from the life of Rebecca McClung, nothing further had been taken. It was also noticed that John McClung's clothing was splattered with fresh blood and that, during questioning, he had mentioned lighting fires in both the sitting room grate and kitchen cooking stove earlier that morning. When asked if he had killed his wife, the old farmer replied, "I might have done it and I might not. If I did, I don't remember anything of it."[127] Lending credence to this statement, interviews with his neighbors revealed that he had been acting strangely for several weeks and seemed to be exhibiting signs of dementia. They also told investigators that the couple had been arguing about a new home they were planning to build on the outskirts of town. He wanted a small abode, whereas she insisted on a large, majestic house. The night before Rebecca McClung's murder, her husband gave in to her wishes and signed a contract for the construction of a fourteen-room home. When she was found dead the next morning, he immediately asked that someone send word to the builders that the project had been canceled.[128] This was all the coroner needed to hear, and John McClung was charged with murder.

Rebecca McClung was buried at Rose Hill Cemetery that Sunday in the cheapest coffin her husband could find, and his trial was set into motion the following day. During the proceedings, it was made known that John McClung detested his wife's relatives and that, as his health was declining, he feared they would become the ultimate beneficiaries of his fortune. One witness claimed that John McClung said he'd convert all his assets to cash and light the pile ablaze before he'd let the in-laws have it.[129] The prosecutor presented this testimony, along with the couple's recent battle over the size of their new house, as a motive for the murder. An analysis of the farmer's blood-splattered suit came back inconclusive, however, which left the state with nothing but circumstantial evidence. On July 11, 1901, the jury ruled that there was insufficient proof to convict John McClung, and the elderly farmer was acquitted.[130] When he died of heart failure three years later, his body was placed in a grave at Rose Hill Cemetery beside his murdered wife. Many contend that the injustice of this arrangement causes her spirit great unrest.

For much of her life, Rebecca McClung had been a recluse, and even though she was one of Mason's oldest residents, almost no one knew her. Whether this was self-imposed or the product of an abusive relationship is unknown, but it even extended to family interactions. Her brother told the court that he had only spoken to his sister a handful of times in the decade prior to her death and that each conversation was held through the closed shutters of a front window.[131] She hasn't been such a hermit in the afterlife, though, and more than a few people have claimed to encounter the slain woman. Many times, these sightings occur within the house where she was murdered, which has been used as law offices, an antique shop and several restaurants over the years. Aside from occasionally manifesting on the second floor in a black Victorian-era dress, she is blamed for a host of odd happenings in the building that range from slamming doors to shattered chinaware.[132] She also is seen at Rose Hill Cemetery.

In late autumn 1938, the phone rang at the Hamilton County Police Department. The desk sergeant picked up the receiver to the voice of a man who was extremely worried about reports of an apparition at Rose Hill Cemetery. He wanted to know if the men he saw patrolling the grounds that night were with the sheriff's department and, if so, might he join them in their ghost hunt. The sergeant told the caller that the police were not involved in any such business, but the man persisted, exclaiming that there was a ghost that haunted the cemetery and that they should assist in rectifying the situation. After a lengthy back and forth with no resolve, the exasperated caller hung up. A few minutes later, the phone rang again. This time, a different person was on the line, complaining that they had seen a ghost roaming the cemetery. Thinking himself the target of a practical joke, the sergeant told the caller that it wasn't a police matter because there

Rebecca McClung's presence is still felt at her former home in downtown Mason. *Author photo.*

The McClung grave site. Rebecca's headstone is at the bottom right of the monument, and John's is the painfully close stone to the left. *Author photo.*

was nothing in the municipal code about punishing ghosts for just being ghosts. Desperate, the voice cried, "Everyone out here knows about it, and something should be done about it!"[133]

Shortly after he retired in 2006, former Rose Hill superintendent Carl Muennich told newspaper reporters of an instance when he, too, thought a practical joke had been played on him at the cemetery.[134] One day, while working in his office, he looked up to see a woman dressed in Victorian clothing standing at his desk. "Do you know where Rebecca McClung is buried?" she asked. Muennich turned around to grab the book of interment records and offer his assistance, but when he looked back, the lady had vanished. Even though her sudden disappearance and manner of dress struck the superintendent as odd, he was certain that the woman he spoke to was very much alive and that he had been the target of a prank. Several days later, that certainty vanished just as quickly as his mysterious visitor, when he attended an event at the Mason Historical Society. While there, Muennich recognized the woman in a photograph. When he inquired about her identity, a volunteer nonchalantly informed him that the photo was of the victim of Mason's only unsolved murder, Rebecca McClung.[135]

WOODLAND CEMETERY, DAYTON

Founded in 1841, Dayton's Woodland Cemetery and Arboretum is one of the earliest examples of the rural cemetery design in Ohio.[136] Its beautiful landscaping and artful monuments, along with the stories of its many famous and infamous residents, make it a fascinating place to explore and take in the city's history. The first official burial there was in July 1843, but in 1859, workers discovered a grave containing nine skeletons that likely predate the cemetery by millennia.[137] In the modern era, it has become the final resting place of humorist Erma Bombeck, Queen of the Roma people Matilda Stanley, and fathers of flight Orville and Wilbur Wright. Out of all the remarkable individuals buried in Woodland Cemetery, though, the grave that gets the most adoration is that of a young boy who didn't amass a fortune, quip witty observations or revolutionize the way we travel. He just loved his dog very much, and his dog loved him back even more.

In mid-August 1860, Johnny Newton Morehouse was playing along the Miami Erie Canal near his father's cobbler shop in downtown Dayton.[138] It was the hottest month of the year, and no one knows if he purposely jumped into the water or lost his balance and fell. All that is certain is that the boy, who was two weeks shy of his fifth birthday, went beneath the surface. His dog, whose name has been lost to history, leaped into the water in a desperate attempt to rescue its friend, but by the time he was pulled from the canal, it was too late. After little Johnny's burial, the grief-stricken animal lay at the grave and refused to leave its deceased master's side. Those who knew about the heartbreaking vigil would take scraps of food and water to the hound, but it eventually succumbed to its sadness.

Daniel La Dow, a local sculptor, was so moved by the story that he created a monument to commemorate the deep affection the child and dog had for each other and donated the statue to the Morehouse family. The touching marker was set in 1861, and aside from the likeness of the boy and his loyal companion above the words "slumber sweet," the tombstone also features the ball, top, mouth harp and little cap that were in Johnny's pockets at the time of his death.[139] In keeping with the tradition first set forth by those who brought food to the sorrow-laden pet, visitors today adorn the grave with toys, trinkets and dog biscuits, which the cemetery frequently collects and donates to charitable organizations.

As heart-wrenching as this tale may be, it may not have been the end for these two chums whose bond was so deep that even death could not keep them apart. Throughout the years, there are those who swear they've seen a little boy playing with a dog in Woodland long after the gates have been closed for the night. One witness who lived across from the cemetery was so convinced that a youngster had accidentally been locked in one evening that they called the police, but a search of the grounds with helicopters and heat sensors produced neither kid nor canine.[140] Others have heard a small child's peals of laughter accompanied by joyful barking where no child or dog can be seen.

Another curious thing about the grave of Johnny Morehouse is that many have asserted that the dog's statue breathes. To their disbelief, those who have put their hand up to the pooch's snout to determine if their eyes are playing tricks on them have felt warm, damp air escaping from the nostrils. While experiencing such a thing must be off-putting, it is a genuine phenomenon and intentional part of the monument's design. To avoid any cracking that might be caused by temperature and pressure changes, Daniel La Dow incorporated a vent in the statue that allows air to escape through the dog's nostrils.[141] It's not ghostly, but if you didn't know and saw steam coming from the nose of a 150-year-old statue in the middle of a cemetery, you'd certainly be forgiven for thinking it so.

Few tombstones elicit a deeper emotional response at Woodland Cemetery than the marker of Johnny Morehouse and his unnamed companion and protector. *Author photo.*

Upon entering the gates of Woodland, one of the first statues to greet visitors is the seated bronze figure of Adam Schantz, a German immigrant who worked his way up from a small butcher shop to become a successful brewery magnate and purveyor of purified water. Over the course of his life, Adam Schantz repeatedly faced setbacks that would destroy his businesses and leave him penniless, but each time, he dusted himself off and came back stronger than before. Two young women had an experience at the cemetery in the early 1980s that suggests death may be yet another obstacle that he has overcome. The women, who were attending the University of Dayton at the time, were taking their usual shortcut through the cemetery on the way to a grocery store. When they neared the plot of Adam Schantz, they noticed an elderly gentleman in an out-of-date suit tending to the grave. Assuming that he was a historic reenactor, the students greeted the fellow and asked about an upcoming tour. The old man responded by looking at them, smiling and then fading away before their very eyes. The women never again used the cemetery as a shortcut.[142]

Another ghost seen at Woodland is that of a young blonde woman patriotically dressed in a red sweater, blue jeans and white sneakers. Like Adam Schantz, she has often been mistaken as flesh and blood, until she

A bronze likeness of Adam Schantz relaxing in a chair perched high above his grave, welcomes visitors to Woodland Cemetery. *Author photo.*

The statue of a young girl contemplating her song at Woodland Cemetery. *Author photo.*

does something spooky, like float through the door of a grave vault. She's usually said to be quite tearful and distraught, sitting atop a tombstone that emits a mysterious, blue, glowing light. The first likely encounter with this mournful phantom occurred during the 1960s, when a man visiting Woodland claimed to hear a woman sobbing nearby. He searched all around but was unable to find the source of the noise. The crying followed him to his car and continued to emanate from somewhere within his vehicle for his entire drive home.[143] The identity of this sad specter, along with the reason for her tears, is unknown.

Strangely, in recent years, another apparition has been seen at Woodland that is dressed similarly to the weeping woman, although she is much younger and not quite so upset. The little blonde girl often appears in the evening near the front of the cemetery and even seems to be helpful, offering directions and reminding people when it's time to go.[144] Like her larger counterpart, the identity of this ghost child is a mystery. Could it be that the same spirit that was so sad as an adult has been able to find happiness in a younger, spectral form? If so, perhaps the reason why she likes to make sure that visitors know when it's time to leave is so that she can play with her little friend and his dog once the living have all gone home.

SPRING GROVE CEMETERY, CINCINNATI

If Ohio's Queen City had a crown, then one of its most dazzling jewels would be Spring Grove Cemetery. Established by the Cincinnati Horticultural Society in 1844, the beautiful burial ground was born from a need to relieve the urban graveyards, which had become overcrowded with victims of cholera. It has far surpassed that purpose, however, and is considered one of the finest examples of the rural garden design in the United States. The cemetery owes much of its greatness to Adolph Strauss, a former groundskeeper for Austria's Hapsburg empire, who was hired to beautify the grounds in 1855. Spring Grove's lush landscaping and stunning architecture combine with the artistry of the monuments to transport the visitor to another realm, and as one of the largest cemeteries in North America, it truly is someplace a person can go to lose themselves.

One of the first sights Spring Grove bestows on living persons who pass through its iron gates is Norman Chapel. Built by Cincinnati architect Samuel Hannaford in 1880, the Romanesque Revival structure currently sees more weddings than funerals. From the 1880s through the early 1900s, the building was also used as a jail, and those who sought the thrill of speeding through the cemetery would find themselves imprisoned overnight within its damp basement cell. In fact, if you were caught going over six miles an hour on the avenue passing the cemetery, you could be dragged into these dismal chambers and forced to spend the night with the dead.[145] These eerie confines must've certainly wreaked havoc on the psyches of those who were locked away here. To this day, echoing screams are occasionally heard emanating from the chapel's lower level.[146]

Not all the ghastly history at Spring Grove is supernatural in origin. In 1889, Mr. Charles Epply, undertaker, was hired to exhume the coffin of Stella Perrin, an infant who had died of cholera thirty-five years earlier.[147] This was done to accommodate her mother's wish to move the body to a family plot in Franklin, Indiana.[148] It also wasn't the first time Stella had been posthumously relocated. She was kept in a vault at Linden Grove Cemetery in Covington, Kentucky, from the time of her death in 1854 until 1858, when she was interred at Spring Grove. A rumor was whispered among undertakers at the time that the child had shown no signs of decomposition in those four long years her corpse had spent above ground.[149] Mr. Epply had

Norman Chapel hosts funerals and weddings, and (as an added bonus) phantasmal cries have been heard coming from the jail cell in its basement. *Author photo.*

heard this story and, while he was exhuming the remains, decided to remove the faceplate of the casket and have a peek for himself. To his astonishment, beneath the glass window lay the nearly lifelike face of the child. Her body had undergone adipocere, a rare, naturally occurring process where fat leaches to the outer layer of the skin, preserving the flesh by encasing it in a waxy coating. The only thing that betrayed the illusion of life was her nose, which lay flat on the face from deterioration of the cartilage beneath. Stella was put on the train and sent to her family plot in Franklin, Indiana, where she presumably sleeps in her remarkable state of preservation to this day.

Another denizen of Spring Grove Cemetery whose image has stayed the hand of time is Charles Christian Breuer, a German immigrant who was laid to rest there in a fine mahogany coffin at the end of August 1908. The preservation of Breuer's appearance isn't due to natural processes, however. It is because of a bronze bust of himself that peers out from the large granite pillar that sits atop his grave. What makes this sculpture stand out from all the other statuary at Spring Grove are its disturbingly realistic eyes, which are said to follow cemetery visitors as they walk past. A long-standing legend has been told that Breuer was an optometrist who requested his own eyes be plucked from their sockets upon his death and mounted into the bust. It's a delightfully gruesome notion, but were that true, the elements, if not the birds, would've made short work of them long ago. As one might imagine, the eyes are actually made of glass, and although Breuer could be called many things, he was in no way an optometrist.

As a young man, Charles Breuer was a butcher by trade, but he grew into an extremely litigious businessman who made much of his fortune through real estate.[150] In 1886, he found himself in divorce court after his first wife accused him of cruelty, neglect and adultery.[151] He then wed his mistress in 1889 and, following her death in 1896, married his housekeeper.[152] In 1905, Breuer abandoned his twelve- and fourteen-year-old daughters from the second marriage, leaving them penniless at an empty apartment in Covington, Kentucky. Meanwhile, he and his third wife lived in luxury at their mansion in Cincinnati's fashionable Clifton neighborhood. When his actions came to light, he attempted to have his children arrested for incorrigibility. He dropped the charges, however, when he learned that the girls had the public's sympathy.[153] During the juvenile court trial that followed, it was revealed that he beat the children, often called them "improper" names and once threatened them with a pistol.[154]

The least damning press Charles Breuer received was the revelation that he kept two mahogany coffins, or "wooden overcoats," at the ready for

The bust and glassy-eyed stare of Charles C. Breuer. *Author photo.*

himself and his wife in a room in the back of their house.[155] The cracks in the veneer of Breuer's sanity became more apparent in 1908. At the beginning of that year, he sent a suicide note to the Hamilton County coroner.[156] The authorities rushed to his home to find him alive and well, although the next day, it was discovered that he had tried to blow up his office building to prevent his daughters from acquiring the property.[157] Charles Breuer eventually reconciled with his children.[158] Soon after, he was back in the spotlight, however, when he issued a violent attack on his wife. It was thought that he likely would've killed her had he not gravely injured himself when he slipped and hit his face against a heavy oak table. After barricading himself in the attic, the blood-soaked madman was finally carted away to Longview Asylum, where he succumbed to the reaper's scythe a month later.[159] Should his spirit truly inhabit the bronze likeness that adorns his tombstone, its gaze is probably one that best be avoided.

One thing that would be hard to not see on a visit to Spring Grove Cemetery is the imposing Dexter mausoleum. This massive Gothic crypt was erected in 1869 for the family of Englishman and purveyor of fine Kentucky bourbons and whiskeys Edmund Dexter. It was modeled after Sainte-Chapelle in Paris and has a manual elevator that was meant to raise the coffins from the first-floor burial niches to the second-story chapel for services. The building's designer, James Keys Wilson, ensured its place in the annals of Cincinnati architecture by incorporating the rather unusual element of flying buttresses. While these are meant to provide the crypt with additional support, Wilson also doomed the structure to a rather limited existence by constructing it out of sandstone, which is a notoriously weak building material. The mausoleum originally had a tall spire at the center of its roof that has since fallen away into the adjacent lake, and the entirety of the building is, sadly, expected to follow suit one day in the not-too-distant future. It has been said that this stunning tomb is guarded by two stark white phantom hounds with blazing eyes of fire. According to legend, they can be summoned by standing on the stairs that lead to the second-story chapel. Sightings of these beasts have been linked with the Cŵn Annwn, spectral canines from Welsh tradition whose appearances are said to foretell death. Given the instability of the massive crypt, it's no wonder these beasts are said to show up whenever someone stands beneath its stone edifice. One day they might not leave disappointed.

The imposing Dexter mausoleum. *Author photo.*

There's a good chance that it was one of Dexter's whiskeys that Mary McDonald was sipping in a saloon near the cemetery on the night of April 30, 1904. When she was found gravely wounded on the tracks across from Spring Grove's entrance the next morning, it was assumed she had drunkenly fallen in front of a train. She was taken to the hospital, where she died shortly thereafter.[160] The theory that she fell onto the tracks was adamantly rejected by the bartender, who swore that she only had two shots of whiskey and was coherent when she left.[161] When it was determined that she had been robbed and a terrible bruise was found behind her right ear, investigators concluded that she had been the victim of foul play. There were no leads, however, and the case was soon forgotten.[162]

Six months later, the body of Louise Mueller was discovered in a clump of weeds at the end of a lover's lane a few blocks west of Spring Grove. This time, there was no mistaking that the girl had been murdered. Two deep gashes extended down both sides of her face, and the base of her skull had been fractured.[163] At the time, detectives believed that Mueller's murder had been a crime of passion and made no connection with the McDonald case. A month later, the grim reality behind these women's fate became clear after the body of Alma Steinway was found just steps away from Spring Grove's front gates. Her head had been bashed in and her body dragged into a grassy portion of the cemetery's southeastern corner. She had been so brutalized that the streetcars drivers thought she was roadkill.[164]

During their investigation of the Steinway murder, police soon learned that multiple women had been assaulted and chased by a madman who leaped from the shadows of the cemetery as they passed by at night. Even Dorothy Hannaford, daughter of the man who designed Norman Chapel, nearly fell victim to the fiend, who was suspected of using one of Spring Grove's many mausoleums as his hideout. The murderer met his match, however, on November 11, 1904. Around 10:00 p.m., Josephine Hewitt was walking by the cemetery when a figure emerged from behind some headstones and grabbed her by the throat. With all her strength, the woman punched her assailant in the left eye and then produced a revolver from the folds of her skirt. At the sight of the gun, the would-be killer hastily retreated into the shadows as the woman fired all six rounds at him. There was no evidence that any of her bullets hit their mark, although the slayings ceased after this attack. For a time, at least.

On New Year's Eve 1909, the remains of Anna Lloyd were found on the railroad tracks near the cemetery. Her throat had been slashed so severely that she was nearly decapitated, and her face had been beaten in the same manner as the other victims. Again, few clues were found.[165] Remembering the horrors of five years earlier, the people who lived in the vicinity of Spring Grove must have been fearful that the bloody slayings of 1904 were about to resume. Just a few days before Halloween 1910, those fears would be justified.

Shortly after 5:00 p.m. on the chilly evening of October 26, 1910, Harley Hackney came home from work to find the front door ajar and the house in darkness. He immediately ran upstairs to check the bedroom and make sure that his young wife, Mary, was alright. The room was empty and undisturbed, so he went back downstairs to search the first floor of the home. As his eyes adjusted to the dark interior of the house, he walked into the sitting room, where he could make out the silhouette of his wife lying against the wall. Thinking that she had fainted, he lit a lamp and bent down to help her onto the couch. As he did so, a scene of horrendous carnage glistened back at him in the flickering light. Mary Hackney's face had been cleaved into sections and her throat slashed so deeply that her head was only attached to the neck by a thin strand of muscle and ligament.[166] Her skull had been crushed and her body mutilated by a series of grotesque lacerations.[167] This time, the killer, for some unknown reason, left behind two significant pieces of evidence: both the axe that they had used to commit the atrocious murder and a bloody fingerprint on the door of the Hackney's home. Unfortunately, nothing came of either clue in the Mary Hackney case, and it, along with the other murders, remains unsolved to this day.[168] It has been speculated that the last killing is unrelated to the others, since it happened indoors and was so exceedingly violent. Yet there are those who theorize that, like Jack the Ripper before him, the Spring Grove slayer chose to go out with one final display of depraved and extreme violence before melting back into the shadows from which he emerged—thus ending the cemetery's tenure as the haunt of a brutal serial killer.

PART III
CENTRAL OHIO

CONCORD CEMETERY, JOHNSTOWN

On a small rise in the rolling farmlands east of Johnstown, there sits a well-maintained country burial ground known as Concord Cemetery. The first interment there was in 1835, and even though it is barely an acre in size, it is still a place of burial. At the top of the hill, in the oldest section of the cemetery, there is a granite obelisk that's slightly off-kilter. Despite its age, this precariously tilted marker can almost always be found adorned with flowers, coins and various offerings. This decorated headstone marks the grave of Sarah Lovina Emerson, a young girl who died more than a century and a half ago but lives on in local memory as the legendary Johnstown Witch.

Sarah Lovina Emerson was born in 1832 and was the granddaughter of pioneers Stephen and Elizabeth Emerson, who came to Ohio from Concord, New Hampshire, in 1815.[169] She died just four days shy of her fourteenth birthday, on August 4, 1846. What happened between her birth and death is a matter of some debate, and locals have been telling variations of how she came to be thought a witch, "as they heard it," for generations. Some folks say that she had violent fits and possessed sinister powers, such as the ability to make a person grow sick and die by simply pointing at them.[170] Others contend that she was a misunderstood girl who suffered from epilepsy or Tourette syndrome.[171] One thing most seem to agree on, however, is that she

Sarah Lovina Emerson's grave. *Author photo.*

died as the result of a fire. Whether this was accidental or intentionally set by those who feared her is another point of contention. The most believable account tells of a deranged girl who spilled lamp oil on her skirt, ran out into the yard and burned to death as helpless villagers looked on.[172] No matter which way she met her tragic end, Sarah Lovina Emerson was buried at Concord Cemetery, where her parents had a poem etched into the headstone that begins:

Young people all as you pass by,
As you are now so once was I,
As I am now you soon will be,
Prepare for death and follow me.

Not surprisingly, some people have interpreted these words as a curse. One dark take on their meaning says that if a young person visits the grave without making an offering to Sarah, they will die before reaching their own fourteenth birthday. Regardless of its ominous tone, this poem was a popular epitaph during the nineteenth century and can be found on many tombstones dating from that era.[173] If it were truly intended as a curse, then there would be few cemeteries that are safe to visit. Also, while it is undoubtedly macabre, the verse is meant to remind the reader of the imminence of death and act as a warning to live virtuously—a message that is hardly the stuff of the nefarious witch of cemetery lore.

A more tangible legacy of the Johnstown Witch says that she is responsible for the spate of fires that have destroyed several nearby churches over the years. In support of this claim, one neighbor reported seeing the apparition of a girl moving through the cemetery and toward a local chapel just before it was consumed by flames.[174] There are very few other reports of Sarah Lovina Emerson's ghost taking on a physical form, although one legend maintains that a green mist emerges from her grave at midnight each Halloween. As unbelievable as that claim may seem, one of the last major church fires in Concord happened moments after midnight on Halloween 1999, when a short in the wiring of a meeting hall sparked a blaze that burned the building to the ground.[175]

Perhaps the most interesting facet in the story of Sarah Lovina Emerson is that she was not the first in her family to be aligned with witchcraft. In

"Prepare for death and follow me." Detail of Sarah Lovina Emerson's burial marker. *Author photo.*

Concord, New Hampshire, where her grandparents Stephen and Elizabeth Emerson were from, a woman referred to only as "Goody Emerson" was once accused of taking the form of a black cat and terrorizing a group of girls in the woods.[176] And in Haverhill, Massachusetts, where Sarah's great-grandfather James Emerson came from, a Martha Emerson was arrested for practicing sorcery and the dark arts during the Salem Witch Trials of 1692.[177] Martha Emerson was released due to lack of evidence, but her father, who was also charged, died in prison awaiting trial. Her mother was likewise charged and confessed to signing a pact with the devil, attending black sabbaths and bewitching a man in retaliation for his attack on another of the Emerson women.[178] Despite this confession, she, too, was eventually cleared of all charges and released.[179]

While it will never be known exactly how Sarah Lovina Emerson died—or if her reputation as a witch was the result of a misunderstood medical condition, some inherited peculiarity of character or just idle gossip—there is one bright aspect to her story. There are those who believe that when her grave is approached with kindness and a gift is given, then she will use her power to help the visitor achieve something they desire. Given the number of offerings that constantly adorn her stone, it's safe to say that if there is any merit to the stories of the Johnstown Witch, then she spends most of her time being helpful rather than hurtful. Although if one was thinking of building a church, it would probably be best to look elsewhere.

GEORGE'S CHAPEL CEMETERY, LURAY

Unless you know it's there, George's Chapel Cemetery is easy to miss. Both the chapel and the sign are long gone, and the only clues that the hillside is more than a cow pasture are a few uneven grave markers, a small section of wrought-iron fence and a curious block of concrete that sits at the back of the field. Less than two hundred yards west is State Route 37, where hundreds, if not thousands, of commuters travel by every day completely unaware of the old burying ground's existence. In the horse and buggy days, most who passed the gates of George's Chapel Cemetery would also rush by without so much as a glance in its direction. This wasn't because they were in a hurry or didn't know it was there, however. It was because they feared what was inside (and, more importantly what might *not* be inside) the imposing box-like structure that overlooks the old graveyard.

George's Chapel (or Luray) Cemetery as it appears today. *Author photo.*

That was before it was encased in concrete and could be seen for what it truly is: a tomb.

The unusual crypt was built in 1847 for James Holmes Jr., an early settler of Licking County who spent most of his life working as a land surveyor for the government. Through a series of successful real estate ventures, he became one of the wealthiest people in the county and during his lifetime was considered a well-respected and prominent member of the community.[180] Yet there was something odd about the old surveyor in the minds of those who knew him. Against the conventions of his place and time, he openly touted a disbelief in Christian teachings, including the concept of an afterlife.[181] While the notion of a hereafter populated with pitchfork-wielding devils and harp-plucking angels seemed ridiculous to James Holmes, decomposition was a very tangible and repulsive prospect that he could not abide. When he took ill with kidney stones, which was then a potentially fatal condition known as "gravel," he was said to have proclaimed:

Shall the worm bore its way through the flesh that is now living and animated, and shall all the slimy snails, beetles, bugs and crawling things

Headstones at George's Chapel Cemetery. In the distance looms the crypt of James Holmes. *Author photo.*

of the earth pass through the mold that was once wont to respond to thoughts and impulses, feel joys and pleasures, sorrows and cares? No, I tell you canting preachers and believers in a senseless creed, I will not have it so. My body shall never turn to dust; my bones shall never crumble away and go back into the senseless clay from which your church people say they have sprung. I will build me a crypt and I will preserve my body for eons and eons of time after heat has left this frame and my course is run.[182]

True to his word, in the months before his death, James Holmes commissioned an above-ground crypt to be built at George's Chapel Cemetery. It was of his own special design and meant to protect his and his wife Elizabeth's remains from the dampness of an earthen grave for all time. He also laid out specific instructions for how his body should be prepared once the veil of life had drawn closed. This was before embalming was commonly practiced, so the methods set forth by Holmes were based on his own experiments in staving off the decay of fruit and vegetables. If the religious community thought his deathbed statements were offensive, then they must have found his funereal plans downright blasphemous. The old surveyor was to be laid to rest for all eternity in a bath of what one church leader referred to as "the devil's own brew."[183]

James Holmes lost his battle with kidney stones on January 13, 1848. In accordance with his instructions, a force pump was used to inject his body with alcohol, then it was placed in a copper-lined black walnut casket with a glass lid and taken to the crypt at George's Chapel Cemetery. Once there, the coffin was filled to the brim with more alcohol and hermetically sealed within the vault.[184] The only other time the tomb was to be opened was to permit the body of his wife, Elizabeth Holmes, to join him. That opportunity came one year later, but it would turn out that she left her own specific instructions, which stated that under no circumstance was she to be placed beside her husband and his spiritous stew. She was instead buried in the traditional subterranean manner just a few feet away.[185] The old surveyor would eventually get company in his crypt, however.

On May 27, 1865, Emily Wigton, one of the Holmes daughters who had since moved away, dropped dead while on a trip home to visit relatives. Her brothers and sisters saw no reason she shouldn't fill the vacancy in their father's crypt. So, in keeping with his abhorrence of decay, they hired an undertaker who had recently assisted in embalming the body of Abraham Lincoln, and her corpse was prepared for the tomb using the latest methods in preservation.[186] When the vault was opened and Emily Wigton's casket was put into place, it was observed with great astonishment that the remains of James Holmes were still intact. His body and the liquid in which it swam had turned a brackish shade of brown, but otherwise he looked as he did on the day of his own burial, nearly twenty years earlier.[187] After the funeral, the crypt was resealed for what was assumed to be eternity.

Word of the remarkable mummification soon spread across the countryside, along with strange stories told by those who were well acquainted with the cemetery. It was noticed that the birds that flittered about the grounds during the summer months would never alight on the old man's tomb, seemingly aware of the affront to death that was contained within. At night, a tall, thin figure would sometimes be seen striding across the hillside, dressed in the clothes of a bygone era and with a surveyor's transit slung over its shoulder. Those who had encountered the specter firsthand said that it was accompanied by a chill wind and that its eyes gleamed in their sockets from behind closed lids. Others who passed the cemetery at night would swear that they heard gurgling and the slosh of wet footsteps, as though the surveyor were keeping pace with them from somewhere in the darkness.[188]

Few who had been told these tales were brave enough to test their validity by venturing near the graveyard after nightfall.

Ghost stories weren't the only thing keeping people away from George's Chapel Cemetery. The nearby village of Luray had enjoyed a boom during the canal and stagecoach era of the 1830s, and as the population grew, so did the cemetery. In the decades that followed, the railroads diverted traffic and business elsewhere, and the town and burial grounds were all but abandoned. The last grave was dug into the hillside there in 1890, and by 1901, the cemetery, which was once considered the resting place of many influential and prominent pioneers, had fallen into neglect.[189] It was around this time that some ghoulish soul decided to break into the crypt and look in on what remained of old James Holmes.[190]

In the summer of 1902, a girl who lived by the cemetery happened to notice as she was walking past that the burial chamber had been opened by vandals. Having often wondered about its inhabitants herself, she bravely crept inside. There she found James Holmes lying in his glass-topped coffin. His flesh was as pristine as had been described nearly forty years earlier, although the alcohol bath had evaporated slightly, exposing a face that had turned a pale gray in color.[191] The corpse was so lifelike in its appearance that the girl said she would not have been surprised to hear a muffled snore coming from the casket.[192] The body of his daughter, Emily Wigton, was also in a state of near perfect preservation. Her black silk dress and lace collar were still fresh and clean, and her face looked supple and full. The only exceptions were her nose, which had slightly flattened, and her mouth, where the upper set of dentures had fallen and parted the lips, suggesting a ghastly smile that bordered on the sinister. After leaving the crypt, the girl had nightmares about her time spent with the dead father and daughter, but she went on to excitedly tell anyone who would listen about her grim discovery.

In time, crowds of sightseers began arriving at George's Chapel Cemetery to witness the spectacle for themselves. On occasion, the caskets were even pulled to the front of the vault so that those who came to do so could more easily satisfy their morbid curiosity. When relatives of James Holmes and Emily Wigton learned of what was going on at the cemetery, they were understandably horrified. In November 1903, the family hired stonemasons to reseal the tomb and encase it in the concrete that surrounds the vault to this day, thereby ensuring that the old surveyor—who so much detested the notion of invading worms, beetles and crawling things—would forever be protected, along with his daughter, from the prying eyes of the most intrusive creatures of all.

CAMP CHASE CONFEDERATE CEMETERY, COLUMBUS

During the Civil War, Ohio contributed more than 31,000 soldiers to the Union effort, the third-largest number of any state in the North.[193] As a result, various training camps were established from Cleveland to Cincinnati and all points in between. The most notable in Central Ohio was Camp Chase, a 160-acre training facility that loomed on a hill a few miles west of Columbus. Over the course of the war, 150,000 Union soldiers, as well as future presidents James Garfield, William McKinley and Rutherford B. Hayes, would pass through its gates. Camp Chase was more than just a training grounds though—it was also a prison. During its lifespan, an estimated 26,000 Confederate prisoners were held there. Roughly 2,260 of them never left.

When Camp Chase was established in May 1861, a single acre was set aside to hold 250 prisoners of war, but as a steady stream of captives poured in, two additional five-acre stockades were created.[194] At its height, the population swelled to more than 9,000 inmates, most of whom were civilian Confederate sympathizers from Kentucky and western Virginia.[195] As was the case in any military prison, conditions at Camp Chase were less than pleasant. The latrines were described as little more than open pits, and outbreaks of diseases like dysentery, typhus and smallpox were rampant. In August 1863, a cemetery was established, and while some of the dead were laid to rest in marked individual plots, many were victims of contagious disease and buried in mass graves.[196] The deadliest period at Camp Chase was around February 1865, when illness, cold weather and malnourishment took the lives of nearly 500 prisoners. Two months later, the South surrendered.

Following the Union's victory, Camp Chase was dismantled, and the scrap wood from the buildings was used to erect a crude fence and grave markers at the cemetery. As the nation's wounds began to heal, an effort was made to improve the burial grounds. In 1886, a stone wall replaced the rickety wooden fence, and in 1902, an arch that reads "Americans" was raised over the cemetery's original marker, a boulder that proclaimed the grounds as the final resting place of 2,260 Confederate soldiers.[197] In 1908, the first of the marble slabs that currently stand were erected.[198] Around that same time, a real estate agency purchased most of the Camp Chase land and divided it into lots for residential development.

The first indications that all was not well at the old military site came from the inhabitants of those early subdivisions. Residents would hear soldiers marching through the neighborhood at night, only to look outside

Camp Chase Confederate Cemetery. *Author photo.*

and find the streets vacant.[199] Interestingly, this mirrors reports by the first families to occupy Ohio's other Confederate prison camp, Johnson's Island.[200] In both cases, these disturbances only occurred briefly and have long since been forgotten, although other, more persistent ghosts are said to linger. By far, the most famous of these at Camp Chase is the phantasmal Lady in Gray.

People have been seeing her for years: a woman in a gray dress, moving among the white marble slabs of the cemetery, weeping as she glides from stone to stone. Those who have attempted to get close have found that she easily outpaces them, and most attempts to get a good look have proved fruitless. There was one cemetery visitor, however, who claimed to get near enough to make out the lines in her long, pleated skirt and see the glint of tears on her cheeks as she knelt at a grave to pray.[201] A moment later, she faded into nothingness. For reasons lost to the living, the Lady in Gray bestows most of her supernatural energies on the tombstone of a Tennessee infantryman named Benjamin Allen and a marker dedicated to an unknown soldier. Fresh flowers that are found at these graves are attributed to her ghostly hand.

Like the unknown soldier she mourns, no one is exactly certain who the Lady in Gray was in life. One theory is that she was a lonely widow who showed up in Columbus a decade after the war to search for her husband's grave.[202] True to her nickname, she was described as wearing only gray and was often seen crying as she walked up and down the rows of graves at Camp Chase, reading and rereading the inscriptions on the rotting wooden markers.[203] Eventually, she stopped showing up at the cemetery, and it was presumed that she either moved on or died of heartache. Since sympathies for the South weren't that strong in Ohio, no one went looking and no one cared. Some believe that even beyond her own death, she continues to search for the grave in hopes of being reunited with her love. Perhaps it's just a coincidence, but around the same time this mysterious widow first appeared, a young southern woman who had been transplanted to Columbus during the war began making clandestine visits to Camp Chase. Her name was Louisiana Ransburgh Briggs.

Louisiana Ransburgh was born in New Madrid, Missouri, in 1849, but following the death of her mother and the outbreak of the Civil War, she was sent to live with her father's relatives in Columbus. From there, she attended a women's college in the nearby city of Delaware. As a young woman, her transition into northern culture was not a smooth one. At school, she would bring her own stool to class to avoid sitting beside "damn Yankees." She often expressed proslavery sentiments, and when word of Abraham Lincoln's assassination reached Ohio, she celebrated in the streets.[204] To put it mildly, Louisiana Ransburgh was not well liked. Consequently, she wanted out of school as quickly as possible, and the best opportunity to do so came in the way of a marriage proposal by Joseph Musser Briggs, a man who was not only twice her age but also a captain in the Union army. He also happened to be the wealthiest man in the area, and despite the differences in their age and political ideologies, she accepted his offer and became Mrs. Joseph M. Briggs on October 16, 1867.[205]

About ten years into the marriage, Louisiana Briggs became upset over the poor conditions at Camp Chase Cemetery. However, she knew that if she were seen laying flowers on Confederate graves, it would be disastrous to her husband's high standing in Columbus society. So, one night, she dressed in her finest Victorian mourning attire, complete with a veil, took a closed carriage to the cemetery, jumped out, tossed flowers over the wall and then quickly returned to her carriage and raced home. With time, Louisiana Briggs became bolder in her visits to Camp Chase Cemetery, although she always donned the veil to maintain her anonymity and preserve her husband's reputation. She continued this practice until her death in 1950 at the age of one hundred. Those who've witnessed the gray form of a woman drift down the rows of stones and then inexplicably vanish or found fresh flowers lying atop a grave where moments before there were none say that she still makes her rounds—although the veil that now separates her from the modern world is far more substantial than lace.

Little Pennsylvania Cemetery, Darbydale

On the outskirts of Darbydale, just a few miles southwest of Columbus, a nondescript steel barricade marks the entrance to a little burial ground with a big reputation. Beyond the gate, a wood-lined path leads to a clearing, past which rows of graves ascend a narrow hillside cemetery. Long ago, this was the site of a Mennonite church, and the earliest burial dates to 1811, making it one of the oldest active cemeteries in Franklin County.[206] Over the course of its two-hundred-year history, it has been referred to as "Green Hill," "London-Darbydale" and "Little Pennsylvania Cemetery." It's also reputed to be one of the most haunted locations in Central Ohio and known to the paranormal enthusiasts who consider it as such by the name "Woolybooger."

At first glance, it would be hard to imagine how this pleasant country cemetery could have such a gloomy reputation. Its soil has embraced pioneers, pastors, veterans and poets—many of whom still have descendants living in the area and tending to their graves. There is seemingly little reason why such a place should be so haunted. Yet countless people attest that they've been witness to eerie apparitions and encountered monstrous beasts in the cemetery.[207] An ethereal young girl in a white dress has long been said to roam there, and ghost hunters have claimed that other, darker forms, some human and some inhuman, have chased them from the cemetery.[208] Even those who are innocently driving past the gate at a late hour have reported unexplained car trouble, feelings of dread and screams wrenching out from somewhere in the forest.

Just how the cemetery got its unusual nickname has long been a matter of speculation. One theory is that it was derived from Willie Butcher, a man who was supposedly driven insane by graveyard ghosts, slaughtered his entire family and then committed suicide at a nearby farmhouse in the late 1800s. Legend has it that after the crime was discovered, townsfolk quietly buried

Once you've entered Little Pennsylvania Cemetery, there is no fast way out. *Author photo.*

the victims in the adjacent cemetery and burned the house to the ground. For obvious reasons, there is no record that such a thing ever happened. In fact, there is no documentation that such a family existed in tax records, deeds or the census. So, if this is true, a round of applause is in order for the cover-up committee. Coincidentally, there is a Willie Boucher buried there, but it's unlikely that he got up to too much murder. He died when he was ten months old.

Another possibility is that "Woolybooger" originally referred to a different burial ground altogether. Hidden in the woods about a half mile west of Little Pennsylvania Cemetery, there is a small plot for the Biggert family. John and Catherine Bigger were Irish immigrants who came to Ohio around 1800, added a *t* to the end of their name and built the first brick home in the region.[209] In 1802, they had a son named William, who, in turn, raised his own family there during the mid-1800s. One of Willie Biggert's sons, James, was declared an "imbecile" in 1877,[210] and in 1898, the Biggert family suffered a devastating barn fire.[211] While there is no indication that any of the family ever committed murder, let alone familicide, it's easy to imagine how the rumor mill of a small 1800s farming community might've spun a yarn around someone who was different and how, over time, the

Little Willie Boucher's grave. *Author photo.*

truth was warped into the story that is told at slumber parties and camping trips today. It's also not a long stretch to imagine how the names of two old cemeteries that aren't that far apart could get confused, and "Willie Bigger[t] Cemetery" could become "Woolybooger Cemetery." Longer stretches have certainly been made.

Some believe that the name "Woolybooger" is in reference to a Sasquatch-type creature that stalks the woods surrounding Little Pennsylvania. Supporting this notion, there have been several reports of glowing eyes that peer from behind the trees at the cemetery's edge. On occasion, these encounters have been accompanied by growling sounds, horrible smells and even sightings of shadowy figures that have chased frightened visitors from the area. Skeptics have suggested that local hunters wearing headlamps and camouflage are to blame for these sightings. To be fair, the area is a popular stomping ground for the outdoorsy type. Independent of cryptids and ghosts, hunting and fishing enthusiasts have occasionally found more than they bargained for in the forest near the cemetery.

In the early spring of 1957, four young anglers stumbled on the body of a woman that had been rolled in a towel, stuffed into a feed sack and dumped on the bank of Big Darby Creek near Little Pennsylvania. As it turned out, she was a twenty-nine-year-old mother from St. Louis, Missouri, who learned that her live-in boyfriend was married to a woman in Columbus, Ohio. When she confronted her beau, he strangled her to death, shoved her body into the trunk of his car and drove to Darbydale, where he tossed the remains in Big Darby Creek.[212]

Another grisly discovery was made on the Saturday morning after Thanksgiving 1979 when two hunters found the corpse of a man that had been bound, stabbed to death and thrown into the pond behind the cemetery. A subsequent investigation revealed that the victim was a car salesman from downtown Columbus who had been murdered by two juvenile delinquents so they could steal a Camaro Z28.[213]

Two years later, a couple on a date in the German Village neighborhood of Columbus were carjacked by a violent kidnapper. The thug repeatedly struck the woman with an iron bar as he forced the man to drive to Darbydale and pull into a turnaround across from the cemetery. Once there, the male victim jumped out of the car and used his own gun to shoot and kill their abductor.[214] In an odd twist, the kidnapper happened to be someone who worked for the man and had plans to get married the very next day.[215] That's a lot of violent death to surround a quaint, rural cemetery like Little Pennsylvania—and then there are the allegations of Satanism.

Like many secluded burial grounds with reputations for being haunted, Little Pennsylvania was plagued with tales of devil worshipers during the

A view into one of Central Ohio's most active haunted locations. *Author photo.*

"Satanic Panic" of the 1980s and 1990s. Even in recent years, cemetery visitors say that they have unintentionally disrupted gatherings of robed fiends performing dark rites who either pursue them through the tangle of graves or retreat into the woods. Mutilated animals have reputedly been found hanging in the trees, and stories have been told that one of the tombstones was used as an altar and repository for human sacrifice. While that rumor has never been substantiated, it is an interesting aside that the stone in question has the phrase "passed into the spirit world" etched into its face instead of the wording that typically precedes a date of death on grave markers. This small detail suggests that the people buried beneath the tombstone were Spiritualists, a faith that attests that the dead can return to visit the realm of the living. Could this be why it was selected as an altar? If so, what were those who used it as such trying to call forth, and even more importantly, did they remember to close the door? With all the strangeness that takes place at Little Pennsylvania Cemetery, it would certainly seem they did not.

GREEN LAWN CEMETERY, COLUMBUS

When Columbus was founded in 1812, its first cemetery was a marshy tract of land north of the town's boundaries that was aptly named the North Graveyard.[216] Within a span of forty years, however, the city had grown to surround the burial grounds, and like many other cities of that era, Ohio's capitol found itself struggling with the existence of what had become an overcrowded, unsightly and inconveniently located acreage of dead bodies. The solution to this problem came in the summer of 1849 with the opening of Green Lawn Cemetery, two miles south of the city.[217] In keeping with the fashion of the time, the expansive grounds were landscaped and designed in the rural cemetery style, and Green Lawn quickly became the favored burial location of Columbus society. Today, Green Lawn is Ohio's second-largest cemetery and boasts 360 acres of peaceful, tree-shaded lots that have become the final resting place of authors, soldiers, politicians and painters. It is also the eternal abode of some less-than-savory characters and, according to some, even a few ghosts.

One of the most visually striking features to first greet visitors at Green Lawn is the small, yet elegant, Gay-Walcutt tomb, which sits near the center of the cemetery. A rumor has circulated for years that the crypt is haunted

The Gay-Walcutt crypt at Green Lawn Cemetery. *Author photo.*

by way of an eerie blue light that emanates from the structure near dusk. This actually does happen on certain evenings, although the cause is not supernatural, but rather the blue and purple stained-glass window that accents the back of the structure. Its inhabitants are Virginia Walcutt and her husband, Harvey D. Gay—both of whom led contented lives free of the sort of tragedy that usually results in a haunting. However, one of Virginia Walcutt's brothers, George Walcutt, was a Spiritualist medium who briefly made a career of going into a trance and painting portraits of the dead.[218] So, if either of them is lurking around their grave site as ghosts, maybe it's in hopes of being put down in oils and pastels.

Not far from the Gay-Walcutt crypt looms Green Lawn Cemetery's famed Hayden mausoleum. This imposing structure holds the remains of just twelve people and is the largest single-family burial chamber in Central Ohio. It was commissioned by multimillionaire industrialist and banker Charles Halleck Hayden in 1904. The mausoleum first came into use on October 30, 1907, when Hayden had the bodies of three of his deceased children removed from their traditional graves and placed in the grandiose tomb.[219] Most likely due to poor weather, the body of another child, five-year-old Peter Halleck Hayden, had to wait in his grave a week longer before

The grand tomb of Charles H. Hayden and family. *Author photo.*

joining his brothers and sister in the crypt. Even though few people know about him, it's interesting to note that on rare occasions, a sad little boy in Victorian-era clothing has been seen sitting on the steps that lead to the mausoleum's entrance.[220]

The most well-known cemetery lore concerning the Hayden Mausoleum is that if you knock on its enormous wooden doors, the Haydens might knock back. The interior of the building is one large octagonal room of marble and glass that is just as much a tomb as it is an echo chamber. Of course, this isn't the first thing that comes to mind when someone goes rapping on the door of a crypt in search of a ghost, but it's a likely explanation for the legend. Aside from the fact that there is nothing otherworldly about an echo, knocking on the door is highly discouraged, as even the slightest vibrations can cause damage to the aged mausoleum's fragile interior. And besides, there are much darker places to visit in the cemetery than an extravagant tomb full of dead rich people who are rumored to enjoy a game of knock-knock from time to time.

One of those places is on the ridge to the west of Hayden Mausoleum, at the unmarked grave of Eva Wagner. The tragedy that would play out there began in 1880, when tuberculosis took her life at the tender age of twenty-three.[221] The loss devastated Eva's father, George Wagner, and he would spend every Sunday in sorrow and lament at her grave. With each passing year, his grief only deepened, and on the third anniversary of Eva's death, he appeared hopelessly melancholy as he bid farewell to his family and shuffled off for the cemetery.[222]

Usually, the mournful father would return home before Green Lawn's closing time, but not on that evening. Instead, he hid himself away until everyone left the grounds and then he returned to his daughter's grave, held a revolver to his right temple and pulled the trigger. The bullet entered his skull but not his brain—it lodged behind his right eye, blinding him with blood and causing the eyeball to protrude from its socket. Stunned but still alive, he groped through the grass for the gun. Eventually, he found the firearm, raised the barrel to his left ear and once more pulled the trigger. Again, the bullet entered his skull but missed his brain, this time taking a downward trajectory through his mouth and burrowing into his neck near the carotid artery. Disoriented and no longer able to find his weapon, George Wagner spent the next twelve hours writhing in agony and crawling through the tombstones along the ridge, slicked by the stream of crimson fluid that poured from his self-inflicted head wounds. When

Green Lawn Cemetery's Huntington Chapel. Dedicated in 1902, the building also functions as a mausoleum. Visitors have reported hearing phantom voices and footsteps. *Author photo.*

cemetery workers found him the next morning, he was lying on the hillside drenched in blood, muttering over and over in his native German, "I want my gun."[223]

Much to everyone's surprise, he survived this attempt at suicide, although a year later, he would successfully drown himself in a Brewery District canal and finally be reunited with his beloved daughter, Eva. Hopefully his spirit is at peace, although it would certainly be understandable if the hellish night George Wagner spent in Green Lawn were to sometimes echo across the grounds of the cemetery, just like the reverberations created by those who go knocking on the Haydens' door.

PART IV

NORTHWESTERN OHIO

GOLL CEMETERY, ARCHIBALD

One of the biggest obstacles in the development of Northwestern Ohio was the Great Black Swamp: a 1,500-square-mile swath of wetland that once stretched from present-day Toledo to Fort Wayne, Indiana. Traveling through the murky, forbidding landscape was nearly impossible, and there were few places dry enough to raise a cabin, let alone grow crops. In addition, disease was a persistent problem thanks to stagnant waters and the mosquitoes that called them home. In the 1850s, a concerted effort was made to drain the marshland, and today, there is little evidence that the Great Black Swamp ever existed, although a few glimpses of the ancient landscape can still be found dotted across the region. One of the best examples of what it once looked like can be found at Goll Woods State Nature Preserve in Archibald.

The park takes its name from Peter Frederic Goll, a French immigrant who first settled on a small tract of swampland there in 1836.[224] Eventually, he amassed six hundred acres, most of which was drained and used for farming.[225] Goll was so impressed with the giant trees that stood in one section of his land, however, that he left the area untouched, calling it the "Big Woods."[226] A tranquil, sandy knoll near the old-growth forest was set aside by the farmer for use as the family burial grounds. The stand of virgin timber was eventually deeded to the state by Peter Goll's great-granddaughter Florence E. Goll Louys, and in 1965, it became the Goll Woods State Nature

Preserve. In the years since, multiple visitors to the park have had uncanny experiences at the family cemetery, and it has developed a reputation as a place where the veil between the living and the dead is at its thinnest.

The first burial at Goll Cemetery is thought to have been an infant born to Catherine and Peter Goll. At night, a mist from the surrounding swamp is said to drift into the cemetery and take the shape of the mother. Those who have seen her say that she can be heard softly singing to her child and then bitterly weeping as she gazes at all the tombstones that bear her family name. She doesn't haunt the cemetery in solitude, however. Her husband, Peter Goll, is also thought to linger there, along with at least one other troubled soul. In addition, visitors have reported hearing strange noises and seeing mysterious lights dance across the graves.[227]

The most widely shared legend about Goll Woods is that the family committed some unspeakable atrocity soon after their arrival in Ohio. As punishment, they were banished to the swampy forest, where they were killed off by exposure, starvation and wild predators. According to this legend, Peter Goll was the last to die, and after the pain of watching his loved ones perish one by one, his tortured spirit became bound to the place, where it now guards over the family plot.

Goll Cemetery at sunset. *Author photo.*

90

While that makes for an intriguing backstory, a quick glance at the dates on the tombstones, along with the quality of their craftmanship, reveal that this tale could not possibly be true. The family line continues to this day, and Golls are still buried there. Also, there is no indication that Peter Goll was an outcast. In fact, he seemed to be quite respected and was appointed executor to the estates of at least two of his neighbors.[228]

Another rumor surrounding the cemetery is that one of the Goll men was hanged here and that he, too, haunts the grounds. In one version of this story, he went insane and committed suicide, and his ghost can be heard roaming the woods making guttural sounds.[229] A different telling of the story is that he shot someone during a card game in nearby Stryker and was chased back to the woods, where he became a victim of vigilante justice.[230] There is no historical record to support either version of this tale, which is understandable since both involve situations that would've likely been hushed up at the time. It's strange, though, that independent of the vigilante story, fresh, dry playing cards have been known to mysteriously appear in the dewy morning grass at two of the graves.[231]

Ironically, many of the tales that have come to surround Goll Cemetery would have been at home in the works of its most notable burial, Ralph Emerson Goll. Aside from writing countless episodes of *The Lone Ranger* and *The Green Hornet*, Ralph Goll also chronicled two of Northwest Ohio's best-known fantastical tales in a federally funded 1941 guide to Bryan and Williams County. One of these was an eerie ghost story about Sam Coon, a trapper who lived near Nettle Lake and possessed a mysterious drum that could bring rain when played slowly and summon the spirits of native chiefs when struck rapidly. Its rhythm is still said to echo across Lake Nettle in the moments before a storm.[232] The other story details the Nettle Lake Monster, an ancient beast of legend that was thought responsible for the deaths of two young men, Philip Knight and John Crum, who vanished from the lake during an 1840 hunting expedition.[233]

All that aside, there is a genuine sense of otherworldliness that can be felt at Goll Cemetery. While standing at the graves of these people who carved their lives out of an inhospitable swampland so long ago, it's hard not to think of how their bodies have gone on to feed the still waters and giant trees that surround the cemetery. Perhaps it's the ancient, unspoiled landscape or maybe it's something other, but being in Goll Cemetery gives the visitor a strange mix of both peacefulness and intrusion, like walking into a nursery while a mother is singing softly to console her crying child.

The grave of Ralph Emerson Goll, who penned many tales of adventure and the fantastic. *Author photo.*

The white, marble headstones of Goll Cemetery glow in the evening light. *Author photo.*

Cholera Cemetery, Gilboa

For the most part, the village of Gilboa is no different than any other small community found across Northwestern Ohio. There are a few churches, the ever-present ice cream shop and a cluster of grain elevators and silos that dominate the skyline on the north end of town. In the shadow of those grain elevators stands the town's unofficial mascot, a sixteen-foot-tall fiberglass bull that many view as a monument to the community's strength. Whether intentional or not, it symbolically gazes toward a field where a handful of stones act as a reminder of the darkest chapter in Gilboa's history, the time when cholera came to town.

At the start, Gilboa had a very promising future. It was platted in 1837, and many of the village's first settlers were skilled tradespeople, such as blacksmiths, coopers and leatherworkers. The goods and services these folk provided drew other pioneers to the area, and by the early 1850s, the town was estimated to have a nearly six hundred residents.[234] There was a tavern, a general store and a hotel that had the distinction of being the first brick structure in Putnam County.[235] In the late summer of 1852, however, all the streets were empty, and the buildings stood vacant as an invisible enemy brought Gilboa to its knees.

According to most accounts, a hotel employee who had just returned from a trip to Sandusky was the first to get sick and die.[236] When it was determined that cholera was to blame, almost everyone who was able to do so fled the village. It was reported that of the forty residents who stayed behind, nearly half contracted the disease.[237] In total, fourteen people died that August, including Gustavus Thatye, a young doctor from Hungary who was exiled from his homeland for aiding in a failed revolution there in 1848.[238] He was the only person in Gilboa with experience treating cholera and was so untiring in his efforts to help the afflicted that he went an entire week without sleep before succumbing to the disease himself.[239]

The dead were immediately placed in rough boxes and laid to rest, with several of them being buried in either of the town's two cemeteries near midnight.[240] It's interesting to note that while eight of the victims were interred in Harman Cemetery, only one is recorded at the old Gilboa burial ground, yet it is the latter that became known as the "Cholera Cemetery."[241] One possible reason for this is the local belief that children who died during the epidemic were buried in a mass grave there.[242] Since five of the fourteen cholera victims do not appear in any burial records, there could be some truth to this legend. Another possibility is that the cemetery's name is in

A lone headstone of Martha Brought, the only victim of the 1852 cholera outbreak known to be buried in Gilboa's Cholera Cemetery. *Author photo.*

reference to *cholera infantum*, an antiquated medical term that was commonly cited as a cause of death of small children during the 1800s. In support of this theory, there were a handful of children's burials at the cemetery in 1848. Either way, after the epidemic, the cemetery was avoided for fear that walking across the graves might "stir up the germs," and the lonely spot soon developed a reputation for being haunted.[243]

Stories began to circulate that children's cries could be heard emanating from the rear of the cemetery after nightfall, and in August 1926, a brilliant red light was seen swiftly moving in the trees and darting from grave to grave. The light was eventually revealed to be the work of a prankster, but the source of the cries has remained elusive and they continue to be heard to this day.[244] In one recent encounter, a woman who was visiting the cemetery decided to leave her sleeping grandson strapped into his car seat while she had a look around. As the grandmother neared the back of the cemetery, she suddenly heard the child crying out. She raced to the vehicle to see what was wrong, only to find that the boy was still there, strapped into his seat and sleeping as peacefully as when she had left him moments before.[245]

The implications of these children's cries still being heard more than a century and a half after their deaths is almost unthinkable. An even more

An intriguing epitaph for the children of James and Catherine French; its closing line "and other friends" may have given rise to the rumor of a mass grave. *Author photo.*

terrible consideration lies in the fact that those who had cholera were given speedy burials, sometimes before it was certain that they were dead. Although it's hopefully untrue, this leaves the possibility that a baby might have been buried alive at the bottom of a mass grave in the Cholera Cemetery, which transcends the horrific into the extremely grotesque.

HARROD CEMETERY, HUNTSVILLE

Ask anyone in Logan County and they'll likely be able to tell you about the Hatchet Man—a fellow who went quite mad some years past and slaughtered his entire family at a farm on County Road 56, between Bellefontaine and Huntsville. Legend says that he was put to death for his crimes and buried alongside his victims at Harrod Cemetery, which he now stalks as a bloodthirsty ghost, searching for his next victim. To punctuate the haunting, his tombstone there gives off an eerie, otherworldly glow at night. The reason it glows is the opposite of otherworldly, however. The stone is said to have a high content of mica, a mineral that is prized for its highly reflective properties and used in the cosmetics industry to make eyeshadow and lip gloss.[246] Also, it doesn't mark the grave of the Hatchet Man—it's for his nephew.[247] That's right, the Hatchet Man was real.

Andrew Hellman, the person who would later be known as the hatchet-wielding ghost of Harrod Cemetery, came to this country from Worms, Germany, in 1817.[248] He was a tailor by trade, but in 1820, he took work as a farmhand in Waterford, Virginia, where he married his employer's daughter, a beautiful and light-hearted young girl by the name of Mary Abel. Initially, the union was a happy one, but dark clouds began to gather over their relationship nine months later when their first child, Louisa, was born. Fatherhood did not bring out the best in Andrew Hellman. He grew hateful and abusive toward his wife, accusing her of infidelity. Things only got worse with the birth of their second child, Henry, in 1823. Rather than dote over his son and pass out cigars, Andrew decried Mary as a harlot and disowned the infant. When their third child, John, came along in 1827, he vowed that he'd kill his wife if she ever gave birth again.[249]

Andrew's dislike for his own family was so great that at one point he abandoned them and moved to Baltimore, but three months later, the tailor from Worms came crawling back home, claiming that he was a changed

Even though Harrod Cemetery wasn't formally established until 1898, it has been a burial ground since 1825. *Author photo.*

man. To help give the couple a fresh start, Mary's father bought them a farm in Carrolton, Ohio. The family moved there in 1830, only for Andrew to return to his hateful ways and refuse to live in a house that was in his wife's name. A rare moment of happiness for Mary came in 1837 when Andrew announced that he had purchased a farm near Huntsville. As luck would have it, the land was just one hundred yards from her brother John's farm and a short distance from where her elder brother, George, lived. Moving near his in-laws was not Andrew's intention, and the proximity of Mary's relations brought about an increased sullenness in his already unpleasant demeanor.[250]

One morning, Mary noticed a film of white powder floating at the top of some milk she had poured into a bowl. Suspicious that her husband was trying to poison her, she tossed it away. In April 1839, her suspicions were again aroused when all three children became violently ill. The doctor was called, and the diagnosis of scarlet fever was announced. Andrew was charged with administering the medication, and it looked as if all three would make a full recovery. Then, on April 20, Louisa, who was just sixteen, suddenly died. The next day, before anyone had time to process the shock of her death, eleven-year-old John followed his sister to the grave.[251] Both were buried at Harrod Cemetery.

Andrew showed no signs of grief at their passing, and it was widely believed that he had poisoned the children. However, the fact that Henry, the one whom Andrew despised the most, was the only child to survive, must have cast some element of doubt on the theory. Still, Mary kept a close watch over her only surviving child, fearful that her suspicions were true and that Andrew would make another attempt to end the boy's life. When Mary's brother George took ill that September, she eagerly sent young Henry to the safety of his uncle's house under the guise that he was needed there to help with the chores.[252] This left Mary all alone with Andrew.

On the morning of Saturday, September 28, Mary's sister-in-law, Rachel Abel, stopped by the Hellman home for a visit. When she entered the house, she found Andrew lying on a bed in the front room, covered in blood. In a strained voice, he told Rachel that two men had come into the house and knocked him out. Rachel immediately ran to the bedroom, where she found Mary's body, which had been brutally hacked to pieces. When Mary's brother George arrived at the scene, he instantly accused Andrew of murder. The allegation was supported when the doctor examined Andrew for injuries but couldn't find a single scratch on his person. He had slaughtered his wife and poured her blood over his head to cover the crime.

The graves of Louisa and John Hellman. Mary Abel Hellman, whose headstone is mostly destroyed, is buried to the right, at the edge of the tree line. *Author photo.*

Mary was buried beside her children at Harrod Cemetery. Andrew was taken to the jailhouse at Bellefontaine, where he spent fourteen months awaiting trial. The cells of the jail were not heated, and on cold days, he was allowed to spend time near the stove in a non-secure portion of the building. On November 13, 1840, he decided to make full use of the lax security and discreetly slipped out into the world through an open door. Deputies gave chase and Andrew was tracked across the state, but they eventually lost his trail.[253]

The Hatchet Man would not make another appearance until April 1843, when a search party was instigated at Reisterstown, Maryland, for Matilda Horn, the missing seventeen-year-old wife of a moody, fifty-one-year-old tailor named Adam Horn. Almost immediately after the search began, her headless torso was found buried in a ditch not far from the couple's home. Tellingly, it had been stitched up in a coffee bag with her husband's name on it. Investigators then turned their attention to the Horn house, where they found a pair of legs also sewn into a coffee bag. The limbs had been well salted, and it looked as though the murderer had cut himself a steak from one of the appendages.[254]

Adam Horn fled town before an arrest could be made, but after being on the run for just a few days, he was recognized and captured in Philadelphia.

Authorities from Ohio, whose suspicions had been aroused by descriptions of the fugitive, arrived at the Philadelphia jail and positively identified him as none other than Andrew Hellman.[255] The State of Ohio tried to extradite Andrew, but looking on their past mishandling of his conviction, the governor of Maryland refused the order and had him first tried there for the murder of Matilda and the unborn child it was later revealed that she had been carrying.

It only took the jury ten minutes to reach a guilty verdict, and on January 12, 1844, Andrew Hellman was hanged until dead at the Baltimore jail. Witnesses reported that he danced the hangman's jig for six minutes before his body went still. After that, the corpse was placed in a coffin and returned to the jail, where doctors used electrical currents to perform a series of *Frankenstein*-inspired experiments on the killer's remains. Once the physicians were done having their fun, the body was released for burial to the only survivor of Andrew Hellman's murderous hatred: his son Henry Hellman.[256]

No one knows exactly what Henry Hellman did with his father's body after he took possession of it. Some claim that he left it behind in Maryland, while others say that he brought it back to Ohio and had the killer's corpse quietly interred beside his slain family at Harrod Cemetery, which takes the phrase "burying the hatchet" to a whole different level. The headstone that bears the name "Andrew Hellman" at the cemetery is most assuredly for a nephew. In a letter written shortly before his execution, though, the murderer alluded to a rumor that the young man might have been his bastard son.[257] Regardless, the Andrew Hellman who was put to death in Maryland needs no stone to mark his grave. The stories that are told around campfires and at sleepovers are far more effective at remembering him for what he truly was: a monster.

RAVINE CEMETERY, SYLVANIA

Death has often been referred to as the "Great Divide," likening it to a deep chasm that separates the living from the dead. At Ravine Cemetery in Sylvania, visitors are reminded of this concept by the thirty-foot-deep gorge that splits the burial ground into eastern and western halves. As one might imagine, it is also this feature that gives the cemetery its name. The ten-acre memorial park was officially established in 1856, although private burials are thought to have been taking place there since as early as 1824.[258]

A row of graves at Ravine Cemetery. The tombstone on the far left is that of Rhoda Hubbard, sister to vicious murderer Return Ward. *Author photo.*

Visitors to the cemetery can find the graves of Betty Boop Fallis, "Freddy" Frederick Kreuger and Nettie Cameson Hollis, a performer with Barnum & Bailey Circus who was burned to death in 1918 when a lamp exploded in her living room.[259] Rhoda Hubbard—whose brother, Return Jonathan Meigs Ward, has arguably been touted as Ohio's first serial killer—is also buried here.[260] However, the cemetery is most known for its resident ghost, whose name has been lost to history, referred to simply as the phantom bride of Ravine Cemetery.

The tragic specter first made its way into the public consciousness in 1970, when a tombstone salesman recounted a tale told to him by a longtime caretaker of the cemetery in the local newspaper, the *Toledo Blade.* The story began in the Victorian era with a respectable young woman who wanted nothing more in life than to get married and raise a family. While still in her teens, she was wed to her childhood sweetheart, but he died just a few years later. Eventually she took a second husband, but he met an early end as well. Not to be dissuaded, she tried her hand at love a third time, but that marriage also ended when her spouse died prematurely. Following the death of her last husband, the sorrow-laden widow gave up on her dream and lived out the rest of her life alone. She died thirty years after her last spouse's passing. Uncertain which husband to bury her with, her surviving relatives chose the safest route and placed the woman in a solitary grave. It is from there that she rises in the morning mist and passes between the tombstones in long, flowing white robes, with her auburn hair illuminated by the emerging sun as she searches out her lost loves' graves.[261]

So, who might the spectral bride of Ravine Cemetery be? Several theories have been put forth over the years, including one suggestion that she is Minerva Starr Stow, the mother of the cemetery caretaker who first related the story of its ghost.[262] Another likely candidate is Eliza Chamberlain Bidwell, who first walked down the aisle in 1848 at the tender age of sixteen. Her husband was a twenty-one-year-old laborer by the name of Erastus Mellen. The marriage produced two baby boys, but it was doomed to fail and Eliza left with the children several years later.[263] Love struck a second time in 1857, when Eliza wed a former prospector and farmer named Harry Bidwell. That relationship was a much happier one. They had three children and operated a large hotel and restaurant in downtown Sylvania, known as the Bidwell Exchange. The couple were famous for the grand balls they held there and were at the top of the town's social scene during the 1870s and '80s. After Harry died on Christmas Day 1885, Eliza continued to run

The grounds of Ravine Cemetery, where the phantom bride is said to roam. *Author photo.*

Eliza Bidwell's headstone. *Author photo.*

the hotel and host parties. Three years later, she married band leader and violinist Bosworth W. Trombly.[264] That was another short-lived relationship, however, and in 1891 she sold her business and spent the remainder of her life living with one of her children.[265] She died on September 4, 1911, at the age of seventy-nine.[266] Unlike the sad ghost of legend, she was buried with her beloved second husband, Harry Bidwell. Also, she had dark hair.[267]

In October 2003, a woman who went in search of the phantom bride with a group of friends had a remarkable experience. As they were exploring the grounds, she looked toward the front of the cemetery and saw a figure in what appeared to be a long, white 1800s-era wedding dress. She watched in amazement as the apparition moved through the rows of tombstones toward the edge of the ravine and then faded into nothingness. As closely as this sighting matches the original legend, the witness reported one striking difference. She said that the bride she saw had dark hair.[268]

There is no way to be completely certain of the phantom bride's identity, and there are undoubtedly hundreds of women who had dark hair buried at Ravine Cemetery. But if it is Eliza Bidwell, then maybe the notion of a tragic soul seeking her lost love is all wrong. Maybe, instead, what people are seeing is a sentimental spirit reliving the happy day in 1857 when she got love right.

JOHNSON'S ISLAND CONFEDERATE CEMETERY, MARBLEHEAD

Situated on the western shores of Lake Erie, Johnson's Island is a peaceful haven for those who enjoy lake life but find the touristy vibe of Put-in-Bay or Kelley's Island too much to handle. The native population who once called the area home had a similar disposition toward tourism. When Epaproditus Bull built the first cabin there in 1811, his plan was to start a village and quarry.[269] Within a year, the local indigenous tribes caught wind of his intentions and burned the would-be developer's home to the ground, sending him and his family fleeing to the safety of Cleveland.[270] The next person to make a go at taming the island was its current namesake, Leonard Johnson. He purchased the land in 1852 and planned to make it a farm, but when the Civil War broke out nine years later, he leased forty acres to the Union army for use as an encampment to hold Confederate prisoners of war.[271]

In the beginning, conditions at Johnson's Island were quite pleasant for the Confederate soldiers, particularly when compared with similar facilities like Camp Chase in Columbus or Camp Douglas in Chicago. Things didn't stay that way for long, however, and in time disease, violence and general suffering became commonplace. Brothers stood guard over brothers, desperate attempts at escape ended with bullets and in 1864 several men were executed for conspiring to set the prisoners free, burn Lake Erie's coastal cities and enact a grand insurrection against the United States of America.[272] By the end of the war, Johnson's Island was described by one Southerner as a "den of horrors."[273]

Once the nation's conflict with itself calmed, the prison was slowly taken down, and today all that remains are a few small earthworks and a cemetery containing an estimated 216 graves. Most of the monuments that currently stand were installed in 1889 and made of Georgia marble. In 1910, a statue of a Confederate soldier was erected at the cemetery, facing the lake in a northerly direction, so as not to imply retreat.

The Confederate dead, like the vanquished indigenous people before them, seemed equally unhappy with attempts to settle Johnson's Island. In the winter of 1877, few people dared to take up residence there. Those who did, however, claimed to hear the clicking and clacking of skeletons in the night, along with the stamp of soldiers' boots marching across the old burial grounds. The hauntings became so much for one family that, like Epaproditus Bull, they fled for the mainland in fear of their lives.[274]

Keeping with the vision set forth by Bull a century earlier, between 1902 and 1916 a limestone quarry operated on the island. It was a successful

A marker for one of the unknown dead at Johnson's Island. *Author photo.*

venture, employing two hundred to three hundred workers, many of whom were put up in ramshackle buildings near the cemetery. In March 1911, the integrity of those structures was put to the test when a terrific storm swept over Johnson's Island. As the buildings threatened to buckle under tornado-strength winds, their inhabitants ran into the cemetery and took cover against the large concrete base of the Confederate soldier statue. Sheltered there from the sleet and rain, they became witnesses to a bone-chilling scene.

It began with a bugle call that seemed to be coming from the dark expanse of the lake. As the sound rang out above the roaring winds, the men jumped to their feet, having sensed at the same moment a movement from above. Looking up, they saw that the bronze soldier towering over them had somehow moved to face the back of the cemetery. As they followed the statue's gaze toward the white marble slabs, they noticed shapes beginning to stir amid the tall, windblown grass. Slowly, the forms took on the appearance of people as they emerged from the shadows and into plain view. Some were corpse-like with hollowed cheeks and tattered gray rags adorning their thin frames. Others appeared neat and well kempt, as though they were very much alive. The workers watched in disbelief as a soldier in the spectral army unfurled and hoisted a Confederate flag above the ghastly troop. At that moment, an eerie chorus of moans issued across the field, and then, in

The lakeside gate of Johnson's Island Confederate Cemetery. *Author photo.*

an instant, they were gone. At this, the terrified witnesses made a mad dash to their houses, conducted a quick evaluation of the buildings and remained sheltered there for two days until the storm finally lifted and they were able to safely cross the bay to Sandusky. Once there, the shaken men tendered their resignations and swore to never step foot on Johnson's Island again.[275]

While this story might seem fantastical, in the years since there have been many reports of strange and unexplainable incidents on the small isle, some of which suggest that it is not just Confederate prisoners who are bound to the place. In the early 1970s, a man who was night fishing along the southern shore heard a rustling in the woods behind him. This was soon accompanied by indistinct voices of what he thought to be a group of men moving in his direction. Suddenly, he heard someone close by say, "Yes, we had one of them over here at one time!" followed by the sound of rifles being unslung and rested against the trunk of a tree. He pointed his flashlight toward the noise and was chilled to discover himself surrounded by nothing but empty forest.[276]

Another possible encounter with the ghosts of Johnson's Island took place in 1995. That summer, a Girl Scout troop was having an overnight stay at a cabin beside the cemetery. Upon their arrival, the excitement of the trip was dampened by gray skies and a constant rain. Despite the gloomy weather, one group ventured out to explore the new surroundings. They had only been gone a short time when two of the girls ran out of the woods screaming. When questioned by the rest of the troop, the terrified ten-year-olds exclaimed that they had seen the ghost of a soldier in a blue jacket on the trail by the cemetery.[277] The shrieking that ensued was probably enough to raise the dead.

Lima State Hospital Cemetery, Lima

On the north side of Lima, in an industrial park bordered by train tracks, there is a low field decorated with rows of aged white wooden crosses. No sign identifies the place, and if one were to enter the fenced-in lot for a closer inspection, they would find that many of the crosses have lost their lettering and are only distinguished from one another by the numbered bricks at their bases. This is the Lima State Hospital Cemetery, and these grave markers are the sole reminders of those who spent their lives mostly unseen, locked away in a living tomb.

When the Lima State Hospital for the Criminally Insane opened its doors in the summer of 1915, it held the title of the largest poured concrete structure in the world and was poised to accommodate more than 1,200 patients. At the outset, this was limited to people who had, as the name suggests, committed a crime while insane. Eventually, however, the institution's purpose was expanded to house anyone the state deemed "untreatable," and the massive complex became a sort of human dumping ground for asylums, prisons and juvenile homes from across Ohio.[278] This led to a situation where innocent people with varying degrees of mental illness and runaway teens with no criminal history were indiscriminately bunked alongside psychotic murderers and sexual predators.[279] Needless to say, these arrangements didn't always turn out well.

Take, for example, the events of March 7, 1928, when a twenty-one-year-old disabled patient, Edmund Riegel, was lured into the hospital's basement and beaten to death with a hammer.[280] His killer was William Mohler, an eighty-one-year-old man who had murdered his wife, dismembered her body and tossed the remains down a well.[281] Despite their vast differences, the two patients had been best friends up until the time of the basement slaying, and the doctors could only surmise that Mohler's actions were driven by his "irrepressible desire to kill."[282] Hospital officials decided that there was little

Wooden crosses mark the grave of patients at the Lima State Hospital Cemetery. *Author photo.*

point in punishing someone of his age, but just to be safe, he was moved to a more secure ward where they could keep a closer eye on him. Riegel was taken to the cemetery, a half mile southeast of the facility.

In the 1960s and '70s, rumors of abuse, rape and murder carried out by both staff and patients at Lima State led reporters from the *Cleveland Plain Dealer* to conduct multiple in-depth investigations of the hospital. The atrocities they revealed were unfathomable. Patients were frequently beaten, tortured and forced into sex acts. Drugs and electroshock therapy were administered as punishment, and a high number of suspicious suicides, overdoses and accidental deaths went unchecked.[283] The criminal investigation that followed resulted in the arrest of thirty-one Lima State employees on charges ranging from assault to sodomy.[284] During the trial, several patients who testified against the staff were beaten upon their return to the facility, and one key witness died under questionable circumstances soon after taking the stand.[285] Despite all this, mounting court cost and the sense that there would be few convictions led the prosecution and defense to cut a deal.[286] Under that settlement, the accused pleaded guilty to misdemeanor assault charges and were returned to their positions at the institution with back pay.[287] Over the course of the proceedings, one prosecutor concluded, "If Hell has a basement, it's the Lima State Hospital."[288]

Victims of these horrors fill many of the graves at Lima State Hospital Cemetery. Beneath one of the crosses is the corpse of a widowed Cincinnati seamstress who found herself in Lima State after assaulting a police officer as she was being evicted from her home.[289] In 1969, the frail fifty-six-year-old-woman died after being viciously beaten by three female attendants in the hospital showers.[290] Beneath another cross are the remains of an infant who was killed when his mother was repeatedly kicked in the stomach by an unknown assailant during the final days of her pregnancy.[291] Afterward, the baby's body was allegedly placed in a mayonnaise jar and displayed on a shelf in the morgue for several days before its burial.[292] The mother, who legend has nicknamed "Apple," committed suicide three years later, and sightings of her ghost, on a never-ending quest to find the baby, were common at the hospital up until its closure in 2004.[293]

By far, the most well-known occupant of the cemetery is Celia "Ceely" Rose, who came to Lima from Pleasant Valley, a charming stretch of farmland outside Mansfield. That is where she had lived with her mother, father and

Ceely Rose's grave at Lima State Hospital Cemetery is the only cross adorned with a photo. *Author photo.*

108

brother until the time of their deaths in the summer of 1896. Ceely was born late in her parents' life, and as she grew up it became clear that her body was outpacing her mind. Even though her developmental disabilities earned her the nickname of "Silly Rose" around the valley, she had a few classmates and neighbors who treated her warmly.[294] One was Guy Berry, a good-hearted and good-looking boy next door who just happened to be near her age.[295]

When Ceely was twenty-three years old, her thoughts turned to matrimony. Not surprisingly, Guy, whom she often watched from her window as he worked the adjacent fields, became the unwitting target of this fixation. Soon she was telling anybody and everybody who would listen that she and Guy were to be married. When news of the supposed wedding made it to the Berry household, they lodged a complaint with Ceely's parents, who in turn scolded the lovelorn girl and forbade her from ever again speaking to her imagined fiancé.[296] Ceely took exception to this proclamation, and on the morning of June 24, 1896, she served her family a breakfast of eggs, bread, cottage cheese with cherries and (unbeknownst to them) a generous portion of Rough on Rats brand arsenic.[297] Her father and brother were dead within a matter of days, but her mother had eaten lightly that fateful morning and slowly recovered. Suspicion soon fell on Ceely, and as her mother regained strength, it is said that the woman, who likely recognized her daughter's guilt, announced that they'd be packing up and moving away.[298] After killing two people to be with her beloved Guy, the idea of being farther removed from him didn't sit well with Ceely, so as soon as her mother was able to eat solid food, she poisoned the woman again, this time with successful results.

It didn't take long for Ceely to be arrested for the murders, and when she went to trial, her mental faculties were almost immediately brought into question. One newspaper even asserted that her insanity was evident from the moment she laid eyes one of her attorneys and called him "good looking"—reasoning that no sane person would ever consider the man handsome.[299] During the trial, Ceely would sing and laugh, seemingly unfazed by the grisly details of the deaths she had brought on her family, and it only took a jury two hours to acquit her by reason of insanity.[300] Initially she was taken to a hospital in Toledo but was transferred to Lima State when it opened in 1915. She died there of pneumonia in 1934, just one day after her sixty-first birthday.[301] A laminated copy of a newspaper photo of Ceely Rose that was taken at the time of the murder trial is pinned to her weathered white cross in the Lima State Hospital Cemetery.

The old mill house at Malabar Farm State Park, where Ceely Rose murdered her family in 1896. *Author photo.*

Strange lights and noises have been reported at Pleasant Valley Cemetery, where the Rose family and Guy Berry are buried. *Author photo.*

After Ceely's death, people in Pleasant Valley began to say that on dark nights a face could sometimes be seen peering from the windows of the vacant house where, decades earlier, she killed her entire family.[302] The property is now part of Malabar Farm State Park, and as recently as 2021, a visitor entered the park office to inquire about its historical reenactor program, specifically as it related to the girl in the old-fashioned dress who they had seen standing in front of the Rose house.[303] There have also been reports of an apparition in the Pleasant Valley Cemetery, where Ceely's family and Guy Berry are interred. The identity of this ghostly figure isn't clear, but it's interesting to note that in his book *The Ceely Rose Murders at Malabar Farm*, Mark Sebastian Jordan recounted a story that Ceely was so well liked by the staff at Lima State Hospital that they once offered to take her on a trip to anyplace she'd like to go. She chose her parents' graves at Pleasant Valley.[304]

There are many claims that Ceely Rose also lingers by her grave in the Lima State Hospital Cemetery. Some have seen her, seemingly unaware of her surroundings, standing beneath the tree that shades her earthen bed.[305] Others have reported seeing shadowy figures in the tree line at the back of the cemetery near dusk, and those who go looking for such things have claimed to capture both visions and voices of the dead at this lonely spot where so many souls have come at the end of their troubled and tortured existence.[306]

PART V

NORTHEASTERN OHIO

TOWNER'S WOODS, KENT

There is something especially unnerving about being frightened in the woods. When you walk into an old house and get an uncomfortable sensation, you can easily convince yourself that it is because the windows are drafty, the door is off-kilter or maybe it was just creaking as it settled. You know that it was made by humans, and most likely, its imperfections are what are causing your feelings of unease. But when you are walking through a forest and suddenly get a sense of dread, then the fear can be much harder to rationalize. Nature made these places, and the things that haunt them are much older than squeaky hinges or banging shutters. They are ancient.

Such is the case at Towner's Woods Park, on the outskirts of Kent, where approximately two thousand years ago a woman was buried on a hilltop overlooking Lake Pippen. She doesn't haunt the park, but rather sleeps peacefully under a blanket of earth, gravel and possibly even a little tar paper.[307] However, she's said to be the reason there is a ghost. According to legend, she was a Hopewell princess, and her grave is protected by the spirit of a fierce warrior who will bring harm to any person who dares disturb her tomb. The most well-known instance of this haunting took place in the 1950s, when a teenage couple supposedly drove onto the mound and fell asleep in their car. Nothing disturbed their slumber that night, but when they awoke the next day, they were shocked to discover the exterior of their vehicle scored by claw marks.[308] Were these really caused by an angered, ethereal warrior? Or could they simply have been scratches the car picked up on its drive through the woods? It would certainly be understandable if they were the work of George Towner, an amateur archaeologist and "fiercely independent conservationist" who owned the land from the 1920s until the early 1970s and considered it an unspoiled gem as well as his own private wilderness.[309]

The burial mound at the source of the legend was first discovered by Towner in July 1931 while he was wandering through his woods and noticed an unusual rock sticking out of the ground. With further investigation, he uncovered what turned out to be a stone axe blade, followed by copper beads, flint projectile points and, eventually, evidence of a cremation burial. The last finding prompted Towner to cease his digging and contact the Ohio State Archaeological and Historical Society.[310] A year later, official excavations revealed eleven distinct burials at the site, including two stone-covered graves that were thought to belong to an "Indian Princess" and a "Warrior Youth." The discovery of the skeletons created a sensation, and throngs descended on the mound to witness the dig.

In an effort to create order from the chaos and rake in a few bucks at the same time, George Towner built a concrete block crypt around the

The ancient burial mound at Towner's Woods Park, outside Kent. *Author photo.*

The sound of drums and singing have been heard rolling across the waters of Lake Pippen. *Author photo.*

"princess" burial, placed a sheet of glass over the remains and charged people twenty-five cents to have a good look.[311] Two days later, a visitor reached into the mouth of the princess and stole two of her teeth.[312] Towner immediately covered the skeleton with tar paper and reburied it.[313] The next year, he conducted a private exploration of the mound and discovered the bones of a child not far from the woman, bringing the total number of burials to twelve.[314] Towner initially planned to convert an old railroad switching station on his property into a museum to display the artifacts, but instead he sold the land to Portage County in 1973. Two years later, Towner's Woods Park opened to the public. In the time since, countless people have visited the mound, yet documented encounters with the ghostly guardian have been relatively far and few between. That's not to say that other reports of the unexplained at Towner's Woods have been any less eerie, however.

During an investigation of the mound in 2009, a group of paranormal researchers who were given exclusive night access to the park captured the sounds of a wooden flute emanating from the darkness of the surrounding forest.[315] Other visitors have heard the faint echoes of singing, chanting and drumming drifting through the woods and across the secluded lake.[316] In addition, the ghost of a pioneer woman who was supposedly killed during a land dispute is said to walk the trails, and over the years, nature lovers and ghost hunters alike have felt a blast of wind accompanied by the rumbling of an unseen locomotive careening along the tracks at the park's southern edge.

While it might seem odd for an uninhabited section of land like Towner's Woods to have such a strong supernatural footprint, it is worth mentioning that just across the train tracks sits Brady Lake, which was the home of a large Spiritualist camp from the early 1890s until the late 1980s. For nearly a century, notable mediums and psychics from across the world gathered there to call forth and convene with spirits of the dead. Although the camp is a thing of the past, the stories that surround Towner's Woods suggest that some of those calls are still being answered.

Saint Johns Lutheran Church Cemetery, Coshocton

Along an old dirt road in the hills of southeastern Coshocton County, a tiny clearing in the woods holds a handful of fallen and damaged gravestones. The little field of broken markers and scattered yucca plants was once a place of worship for a family of German immigrants who came to the area in the 1830s. Over the years, the descendants of these people scattered, the church they had built crumbled into ruin and the graveyard fell into neglect. In the 1960s, the surrounding land became part of a large-scale strip mining operation and the out-of-the-way spot became a haunt for the curious, the bored and the angst-ridden. They were drawn to the old burial ground by a wicked legend that had been passed down from generation to generation. It is a tale of cruelty, murder, revenge and witchcraft, and at its heart is a woman named Mary Stockum.

The most common telling of the story goes that Mary and her husband had nine children, the youngest of whom was disabled. Rather than suffer any inconvenience or stigma in caring for the child's needs, Mary's husband decided to go deep into the woods and murder the toddler. The crime was discovered, however, and he was hanged for the offense. After this, Mary grew twisted and spiteful. She vowed to avenge her husband's death by murdering their remaining children and proceeded to poison them one by one.

When members of the town council realized what was happening, they became convinced that Mary was a witch and burned her at the stake, but even after her death, the surviving children continued to waste away and die. This left the council with no choice but to dig up Mary's corpse, chop off the head and rebury it at a distance from the body. Then her decomposing form was bound in its coffin with heavy chains and returned to the grave.

Once this grim task was completed, the deaths stopped, and things returned to normal, except for at the old country graveyard where Mary Stockum was buried. Those who passed by the lonely cemetery at night would claim to hear a woman's screams and rattling chains. Occasionally, these noises would be accompanied by Mary's misty form gliding through the burial ground in search of her severed head. The veracity of this legend is said to be supported by the presence of two tombstones for Mary Stockum at the cemetery: one to note her body's grave and another in the woods to mark the spot where they buried her head.

It's an impressive tale, no doubt, although the historic record paints quite a different picture. The Mary Stockum of legend was born Anne Maria Lutzen on September 27, 1820. On Christmas Eve 1839, she married Christopher Stockum, and the couple settled on his parents' land in southeastern Coshocton County, where they did indeed raise nine children.[317] After a life of farm work, housework and constant pregnancy, Mary Stockum died on August 29, 1863, just a few weeks shy of her forty-third birthday. Her cause of death has been lost to history, although two members of the extended family died that same week, which raises the possibility that infectious disease was at play. She certainly wasn't burned alive for poisoning her own children in some warped attempt to avenge her husband's execution. Christopher Stockum outlived her by fifteen years, and all nine of their children survived both parents into adulthood—a rare feat for the time.

So, if the Stockum family led such a child murdering- and witchcraft-free lifestyle, where did the tale come from? In 1967, the *Coshocton Tribune* interviewed the cemetery's caretaker, who offered a rather banal explanation for the legend of the headless ghost. He admitted that Mary Stockum had two tombstones but stated it was because the marker had been replaced and when the new one was erected the original was left leaning against the fence.[318] It's a tidy answer, but it seems unlikely that a simple tombstone upgrade could lead to a legend involving murdered children, a hanged man and the decapitated corpse of a burnt witch whose wailing ghost wanders the graveyard at night.

In the book *History of Coshocton County, Ohio: Its Past and Present, 1740–1881*, there is a very interesting section that seeks to describe the day-to-day life of the early pioneers in the region. Aside from the expected stories of raising

The grave of Mary Stockum, whose epitaph reads, "Yet again we hope to meet thee when the day of life has fled: Then if Heaven with joy to greet thee, where no farewell tear is shed." *Author photo.*

Could the headstone of Eva Maria Stockum, mother-in-law of Mary Stockum, be responsible for the legend of her two graves? *Author photo.*

Vandalized grave at Saint Johns Lutheran Church Cemetery. *Author photo.*

cabins, cultivating farms and distilling whiskey, there is an account of a man who went to his barn one morning, only to find that one of his oxen had been "witch-ridden." The beast lay exhausted, with bruises and heel marks in its sides and tears at the corners of its mouth, indicating to the farmer that someone had driven his animal aggressively and cruelly during the night. It goes on to tell of other evidence that witches existed in the area:

> *People who were objects of the witch's spite found a brood of downy young chicks in their chests and piles of sprawling kittens under the half-bushel; and they overheard deep, cavernous voices and fine, piping ones in conclave at midnight up in the air and the tree-tops and under the dead leaves and beside the chimney; and tracks, with a cloven foot among them, were discernable.*[319]

Clearly, then, stories of witchcraft are part of the area's history. Because of this, it isn't too difficult to imagine that there might have been some who had their suspicions about Mary Stockum, and when a series of deaths fell upon the family in a short period, it started a chain of gossip that passed down through the decades, eventually morphing into the legend that is told today.

Despite the facts of Mary Stockum's life, the rumor of witchcraft has left a stain on the rural cemetery. Nearly every tombstone lays toppled, broken or desecrated in some way and beer cans and liquor bottles can often be found littering the site. Like several other burial grounds mentioned in this book, there is also evidence that sinister practices have taken place there. In the 1970s, police reported finding the bodies of six dogs hanging in the trees of the cemetery, and one morning, a lantern, shovel and partially opened grave were discovered.[320] The massive destruction and desecration at Saint Johns Lutheran Church Cemetery are unfortunate reminders that it's not always the living who need fear the dead at haunted burial grounds, but rather the dead who need protection from the living.

SAINT MARY'S OF MORGES CEMETERY, MORGES

If you've never heard of Morges, Ohio, it would more than understandable. It's practically a ghost town. This wasn't always the case, however. It was founded in 1831 and for the first twenty years of its existence was a thriving stagecoach town on the route between Canton and Steubenville. At its peak, it boasted two hotels, three saloons and a population of nearly 1,600 residents. The rising prominence of rail travel led to the village's decline through the last half of the nineteenth century, and all that remains today is an intersection surrounded by a few houses, a church and a cemetery.

The area was predominantly settled by Italian immigrants, and in 1828, the first Catholic Mass was held in the log cabin of Morges's cofounder, John Waggoner. A few years later, Waggoner donated land on the east side of the village for the construction of a church, and in 1851, a brick building was erected on the site. A two-story rectory was added in 1855, and that same year, the church took the name it goes by to this day: Saint Mary of the Immaculate Conception. The yard beside the church and rectory has been a repository for Morges's Catholic corpses since 1830, with the first recorded burials being two teenagers that June.

Over the years, tales have circulated that unusual things walk the grounds of the churchyard after nightfall. One of those wandering beings is thought to be the remnant of a traveling salesman who had been murdered while passing through the area many years ago. It is said that this phantom peddler appears on moonlit evenings, moving through the tombstones with his heavy pack in tow. Rumors of murdered peddlers have provided fuel for ghost stories throughout Ohio, although this one is substantiated in a letter by Adam Burwell, whose family moved to Morges in 1875:

> *There was a tavern and two saloons in Morges at that time. That old tavern was still standing when I was a kid. It had a closet or dungeon as it was called at the time. It had a trap door but no steps. Quite all of the pack peddlers who stopped there disappeared forever. I played hide with the other boys and often we would rope down into it. There were quite a few bones on the bottom and they were human bones. I will not mention any of the names of the folks who operated it at that time, but I know, through granddad's diary, of course. The farmers were not robbed as they had their teams and if they had not arrived home they would have been looked after, but the peddlers were all strangers and not missed.*[321]

While this account goes a long way toward answering the question of whether peddlers had been murdered in the area, it doesn't explain why the specter of one would haunt the graveyard. Perhaps the ghost belonged to an unfortunate traveling salesperson who had been done away with and discreetly slipped into a fresh grave before the advent of the tavern's "dungeon." Or maybe they were killed at the tavern and their spirit ventured to the graveyard for some company. You see, the peddler does not haunt the burial grounds at Saint Mary's alone.

One night, a few men who were coon hunting in the woods near the church claimed to find something much more elusive than a woodland animal. As they tromped through the forest, the hunters' dogs suddenly ran and began alerting at the trunk of a large pine tree that stood along the edge of the graveyard. The men, in turn, gave chase. When they reached the dogs, one hunter shined his lantern upward and scanned the dark interior of the tree for the reflective glint of a raccoon's eye. Instead, his light revealed something that would haunt him until the end of his days. There, sitting among the branches on that dreary night, illuminated only by the lantern's glow, was one of his closest friends—a man who had died and was buried in that graveyard five years earlier. The startled hunter stepped back and told his hunting companion what he had just seen. With great trepidation, his fellow hunter raised a lantern toward the tree, but to his relief he saw neither shade nor beast. Despite this, the dogs continued to aggressively bound at the trunk of the pine until they were dragged away by the bewildered men.[322]

The ghosts of Saint Mary's graveyard seemed to be most drawn to Father Bernard Karjovich, who oversaw the parish from 1960 to 1967. On several

The graveyard at Saint Mary's of Morges. *Author photo.*

occasions, Father Karjovich claimed to be visited by the headless spirit of a girl he estimated to be about four years old. Because of her old-fashioned dress, he pondered if she might not be one of the graveyard's early child burials—their barely legible tombstone has the phrase "died mysteriously" etched onto its face.[323]

The most frequently seen apparition during Father Karjovich's time at the rectory wasn't a person, but a surplice—a white vestment worn by the clergy. The garment would move through the churchyard, as though it were supported by a form that was not visible to the human eye. Father Karjovich had an opportunity to examine the phantom surplice up close one evening when it came into the rectory through the back door and ascended a flight of stairs to the building's second floor. After this, strange noises would constantly be heard emanating from the upper level of the house. One could theorize that this might be the ghost of John Waggoner, the farmer who hosted the area's first Mass in his log cabin, donated the land for the church and graveyard and, incidentally, died while working on the roof in 1871.[324]

Father Karjovich developed a different take on who was haunting the rectory when he saw a huge black snake slither across the floor of his bedroom one night. He took this as a sign that it was not deceased

The rectory of Saint Mary's, where an exorcism was performed in the 1960s. *Author photo.*

parishioners or priests that he had been seeing, but something far more insidious. Following his run-in with the serpent, Karjovich sent for two priests who were specialists in expelling demons. The clergymen stayed at the rectory for several days while performing the rites of exorcism, and both heard the weird noises that had been plaguing Father Karjovich but saw no ghosts. After the ritual, all unusual activity ceased, and in the years since, the haunting of Morges graveyard and rectory have all but been forgotten.

CHESTNUT GROVE CEMETERY, ASHTABULA

It was the Friday after Christmas 1876, and an atmosphere of good cheer filled the No. 5 Pacific Express Train as it plowed through banks of snow on its way from Buffalo to Cleveland. Children played in the aisles, honeymooners exchanged adoring glances and new friends chatted merrily over games of cards in the smoking cabin. Any thoughts of the blizzard that raged outside were melted from their minds by the cozy fires that burned in the stoves of the elegant coach cars.[325] Meanwhile, a group of people gathered at the train depot in Ashtabula, patiently awaiting the locomotive's arrival, which had been greatly delayed by the storm. When they finally heard the steam engine's whistle at 7:30 p.m., they rushed onto the platform, where some prepared to welcome loved ones and others said their goodbyes as they readied for departure. Neither of these things would happen.

Less than a quarter of a mile to the east, the Pacific Express cruised across a bridge that spanned the gorge of the Ashtabula River. Just as the first of the train's two steam engines neared the western edge of the ravine, its conductor heard a sharp *crack* and felt the locomotive being pulled backward. Instinctively, he threw the throttle wide open, and his car lurched ahead so violently that it broke free from the rest of the train. After his engine safely reached solid ground, the stunned conductor looked behind him just in time to see the bridge buckle and the second locomotive descend into the crevasse. He then watched in horror as, one by one, the baggage, passenger and sleeping cars careened off the tracks into the valley below.[326] The scene that would play out there was beyond anyone's worst imagining.

Most of the coaches were torn apart on impact, trapping their occupants in a tangle of splintered wood and twisted metal. Some of the holiday travelers were run through or crushed to death, others were thought to have drowned in the shallow waters of the Ashtabula River and many of the living were mutilated in some way or another by the wreckage. While the shocked survivors who were able to do so pulled themselves free from the crumbled remains of the train, the stoves and gas lamps that had been such a source of comfort minutes before ignited a series of small fires. Fed by the storm's strong winds, the flames quickly spread, and the low groans of the wounded were soon replaced by the agonizing shrieks of the dying.

The sounds of the train wreck could be heard for nearly a mile in all directions, and townsfolk rushed to the scene, guided only by the cacophony of screams and a flickering glow on the horizon. Once there, they found their rescue efforts hampered by the steep walls of the gorge and waist-deep snow that had accumulated on the creek bed. Those who did manage their way down to the disaster site became witness to unspeakable nightmares. Blackened heaps that resembled nothing human lay scattered about the valley, their true nature only revealed by the occasional presence of fire-whitened tooth and bone.[327] Bloodcurdling shrieks and wails rent out from the mangled remnants of the train, and the nauseating stench of roasting human flesh filled the air. One woman who was pinned down in a burning

An engraving from Stephen Denison Peet's 1877 book, *The Ashtabula Train Disaster. Courtesy of Tim Evanson, Ashtabula Railroad Disaster—SD Peet 1877, October 13, 2018, photograph, https://flickr.com/photos/timevanson/45291306631.*

car cried desperately for rescuers to use their axes to chop off her legs but was consumed by the inferno before she could be reached.[328] Another who had been pulled from the train stood beside the river in a state of shock, proclaiming that she could hear her daughter's voice in the din. A man rushed to save the child, only to find her impaled on jagged timbers, engulfed in flames and screaming, "Help me, Mother!" as she perished.[329]

The fire department arrived approximately forty-five minutes after the bridge collapsed, but rather than fight the blaze, the chief and his crew were instructed to let it continue to burn and instead assist in pulling survivors to safety.[330] The company that managed that section of tracks, the Lakeshore and Michigan Southern Railway, was accused of sending this order with the thought that it would avoid paying out claims to families of the dead if their remains could not be identified.[331] Later developments would hint that the corporation might indeed have been capable of such a sinister strategy, although the blame was mostly pinned on the village fire chief, G.W. Knapp, who has long been portrayed as an addlebrained and inept alcoholic.[332]

Since the railroad didn't keep close watch of who entered and departed the train at each stop along the route, it was never firmly established exactly how many passengers were aboard at the time of the tragedy, although it's typically estimated that around ninety-two people died that night. Ashtabula's freight house was turned into a makeshift morgue, where the public could sift through the collection of body parts and relics in hopes of identifying their missing loved ones. The remains of those who were charred beyond recognition were buried at the village's Chestnut Grove Cemetery on January 19, 1877.[333] Today, a thirty-seven-foot-tall granite obelisk marks the spot.

On the night of the disaster, the chief engineer for the railroad, Charles Collins, took a train from Cleveland to Ashtabula, where he was reported to have wept like a child at the sight of the carnage.[334] Although the bridge was designed by the company's president, Amasa Stone, Collins was responsible for the integrity of the railroad's trestles and was overcome with guilt.[335] He was found dead at his Cleveland residence the day after the unclaimed bodies of those who died in the bridge collapse were buried in Ashtabula. His death was initially ruled a suicide, although two separate examinations of his remains would later determine that he had been murdered.[336] He was interred in a crypt at Chestnut Grove Cemetery, just steps away from the victims of the disaster.

The mausoleum of Charles Collins. *Author photo.*

The large obelisk to the right marks the mass grave of the unrecognizable dead from the Ashtabula train disaster. Charles Collins's mausoleum is to the far left. *Author photo.*

At this cemetery on a hill, caretakers, visitors and mourners alike have long reported spectral figures wandering the grounds with luggage in tow, seemingly unaware of what has happened to them. They linger near the mass grave and appear as if they are flesh and blood, only to dissipate into nothingness when approached.[337] One of the sadder of these apparitions is an elderly man in a top hat, who is said to be searching for his grandson.[338] Another melancholy ghost is Charles Collins, who many claim stands by his crypt sobbing and wringing his hands in anguish over the part he played in the deaths of so many innocent people. Perhaps the most unnerving aspects of the haunting at Chestnut Grove Cemetery, though, are the distant screams and cries for help that have been reported by various ghost hunters over the years.[339] The numerous encounters and variety of evidence collected at Chestnut Grove lead many to consider it one of the most haunted cemeteries in Ohio.

LAKE VIEW CEMETERY, CLEVELAND

It may not be the largest or the oldest, but few burial grounds in Ohio can surpass the grandeur of Lake View Cemetery in Cleveland. Established in 1869, Lake View became popular among the city's upper and middle class during the booming Gilded Age. As a result, its monuments are some of the most exquisite and expensive in the state, if not the nation. Granite obelisks rise from the hills, marking the graves of such titans of industry as John D. Rockefeller, America's first billionaire, and Amasa Stone, the railroad mogul behind the Ashtabula train disaster. Here there are monuments to Alan Freed, the disc jockey who coined the term "rock and roll," as well as lawman Eliot Ness and Garrett Morgan, the inventor of the gas mask and the three-color traffic light. Graceful statues remembering the lives of artists, innovators and soldiers too numerous to mention rest against a beautifully landscaped backdrop at every turn, and in the spring, the flowers of the famous Daffodil Hill bursts forth in a celebration of life's splendor. The anchor of Lake View, however, is a 180-foot tower of Ohio sandstone that sits at the highest point on the grounds. It holds the body of the twentieth president of the United States, James A. Garfield, who, if you believe the stories, is the cemetery's least restful resident.

James A. Garfield took office in March 1881, and his administration started off strong. Unfortunately, he was struck down by the bullet of a crazed assassin on July 2, 1881, just four months into his presidency. The attack wasn't fatal, but the infection that followed would be. The newly appointed president lingered in a state of agony for seventy-nine days before he finally succumbed to the reaper's scythe that following autumn. After his death, the body was brought to Lake View Cemetery, where it was temporarily held in the crypt of architect Levi Scofield while a tomb befitting a pharaoh was constructed to honor the fallen civil servant.[340]

The James A. Garfield Memorial was dedicated to great fanfare on Memorial Day 1890. It's a magnificent structure that is outwardly adorned with dog-inspired gargoyles and terra-cotta panels that depict the president's life and death. Near the top of the tower, there is a balcony that overlooks Cleveland and forty miles of Lake Erie shoreline. Inside there are beautiful stained-glass windows representing the original thirteen colonies, a huge marble statue of Garfield, a memorial hall, a ballroom, the crypt that holds the caskets of the president and his wife, Lucretia, and, according to some, a ghost.[341]

A certain degree of peculiarity should be expected at the monument. After all, James and Lucretia Garfield aren't buried or even interred in sarcophagi. They're just lying inside bronze coffins down in the building's crypt, and guests can get within a few feet of the regally displayed remains. Sightings of full-bodied apparitions are rather rare, however. The paranormal experiences here have mostly involved odd glimmers of light or strange sensations when entering the mausoleum. The best-documented encounter with the president's ghost at Lake View concerns a phone call that was received by Cleveland firefighters in 1979. The caller, who claimed to be President Garfield himself, rang the fire department to express concern over an eruption of flames at the cemetery. When his worry was met with incredulous laughter, the voice responded, "But I did not say that the fire had already happened—it is *going* to happen." Ten days later, the roof of a maintenance building did indeed catch fire.[342]

It would make sense that James A. Garfield might develop a ghostly reputation in death. His life was intertwined with the supernatural. His grandfather James Ballou was considered an adept psychic referred to as "James the Clairvoyant," and when he was a teenager, Spiritualism began its rise to prominence.[343] At nineteen, he attended a séance conducted

The 180-foot-tall Garfield Memorial is the largest tomb in Ohio. *Author photo.*

A sculpture carved by Joseph Carabelli for the Peck family. Carabelli owned the Lakeview Granite & Monumental Works, whose employees formed Cleveland's Little Italy neighborhood. *Author photo.*

by Leah Fox, one of the sisters whose reputed ability to receive messages from the dead incited the Spiritualism movement. During the session, he was convinced that his father, who had died when he was an infant, had communicated with him through a series of rappings.[344] In her 1885 book, *The Missing Link in Modern Spiritualism*, Leah Fox wrote that James A. Garfield had attended many of her séances,[345] and even in the White House he confided that his father's spirit guided his decisions.[346] Perhaps he also had a touch of his grandfather's foresight. At the end of June 1881, Garfield called his secretary of war, Robert Todd Lincoln, into the Oval Office to discuss the assassination of his father, former president Abraham Lincoln. It seemed that this conversation was spurred by a recent vision that Garfield had in which he was murdered.[347] He was shot two days later.

In an interesting turn, President Garfield likely would've survived the shooting if it weren't for his doctors, who inserted their unwashed fingers into his wound, poking around the right side of his kidney, liver and pancreas in an unsuccessful effort to locate and remove the bullet. The projectile, it turned out, was on his left side near his spinal column, and it was the infection that resulted from their probing that carried Garfield into oblivion. Even his crazed would-be assassin, Guiteau, proclaimed before he was executed, "Yes, I shot the President, but his physicians killed him."[348]

All that abdominal prodding of President Garfield's innards recalls another notable Lake View resident whose legacy, although not ghostly, is equally stomach-turning. Just a stone's throw away from Daffodil Hill, visitors can find the grave of James Henry Salisbury, a Civil War physician whose claim to fame came about in his attempt to cure the chronic diarrhea many soldiers experienced as they undertook the long march to battle.[349] His solution was a diet of coffee and "muscle pulp of beef," which he suggested should be mashed, formed into cakes and then broiled.[350] Apparently it worked, although his patients felt that calling the dish something less repugnant might make it much easier to swallow, and thus "Salisbury steak," the staple of cafeteria and TV dinners, was born.[351]

Speaking of culinary mavericks, in 1868 Clevelander John Haserot patented a revolutionary device that could slice bread with uniform thickness.[352] The invention didn't result in the cut loaves that can be found in stores today, but it seemed to firmly plant his family's foot in the food

A large boulder marks the plot of Dr. James Salisbury, inventor of the Salisbury steak. *Author photo.*

Herman Matzen's chilling masterpiece, *The Angel of Death Victorious*. *Author photo.*

service industry. Twenty years later, his sons Samuel and Francis Haserot established the Haserot Grocery Company, a successful canning and distribution venture that would grow to have affiliations extending to all corners of the globe.[353]

When Francis Haserot's wife, Sarah, died after suffering a seizure, he commissioned the talented sculptor Herman Matzen to create a marker for the family plot. What the artist came up with is one of the most visually striking and powerful mortuary memorials in the entire state, a monument titled *The Angel of Death Victorious*. The sculpture was completed in 1923 and installed at the Haserot family plot in 1924. The concept for the famous statue was first revealed twelve years earlier, when the *Plain Dealer* ran a feature on Herman Matzen. In the article, the sculptor proclaimed that he meant for the angel to represent "the end" and that he "tried not to suggest in this anything beyond."[354] Despite its nihilistic roots, the sculpture elicits a visceral response in all who view it. The angel sits on a granite base with outstretched wings and hands resting on an inverted torch as its black, vacuous eyes stare from a cold, tear-stained face. To learn that the statue is considered haunted should come as no surprise.

There are those who say it sometimes turns its head to follow as the living walk past. Others claim they've watched real tears stream down its cheeks. A few believe it rises from its granite base and wanders the cemetery at night, and one legend says that anyone who touches it will die soon after. Conversely, some see the angel as a guardian figure and leave offerings and gifts in hopes that it will watch over their deceased loved ones. It has even been speculated that Herman Matzen imbued the statue with consciousness as he created it, like the story of Geppetto and Pinocchio.[355]

On that last point, the artist did believe in the supernatural, and it does feel as though the angel *sees* you as you stand before it, although in his own words, the sculpture was not created to suggest the existence of any such thing. It merely signifies the end.[356] Still, in its attempt to convey a single message, it speaks a million words in a multitude of languages, and like every ghost story ever told, its meaning and truth lie in the heart of the observer. Only one fact exists outside the realm of interpretation: when the pages of this book have turned to dust and the eyes that read them have become hollow sockets, the Angel of Death will remain victorious.

NOTES

Introduction

1. *Daily News-Tribune* (Greenville, OH), August 12, 1922; *Chillicothe (OH) Gazette*, October 19, 1922.
2. FamilySearch, "Ohio Deaths, 1908–1953," database with images, https://familysearch.org/ark:/61903/1:1:XZ41-TY4, Henry Lipinstock, August 2, 1922, citing Leroy, Lake, Ohio, reference fn 43876, FHL microfilm 1,992,066.
3. *Cleveland Plain Dealer*, August 13, 1922.
4. *Cleveland Plain Dealer*, April 19, 1923.
5. FamilySearch, "Ohio Deaths, 1908–1953," Henry Lipinstock.
6. Raymond S. Baby, "A Unique Hopewellian Mask—Headdress," *American Antiquity* 21, no. 3 (1956): 303–4.
7. William F. Romain, *Shamans of the Lost World: A Cognitive Approach to the Prehistoric Religion of the Ohio Hopewell* (Plymouth, UK: Altamira Press, 2009), 120–22.

Part I

8. Despite this proclamation, in *History of Marietta*, Thomas J. Summers wrote that Dr. Manasseh Cutler found an adult skeleton near the summit of the mound when he conducted a brief exploration of the structure

in 1788. *History of Marietta* (Marietta, OH: Leader Publishing Company, 1903), 302–3.

9. Ibid., 305–6. This includes an account of General Benjamin Tupper, who was buried under an apple tree between Third and Fourth Streets.

10. Wikipedia, "Abraham Whipple," last modified November 5, 2021, https://en.wikipedia.org/wiki/Abraham_Whipple.

11. Linda Showalter, "Marietta College Library Special Collections," *Pioneer Prologue: Sally Dodge Cram Green, a Restless Spirit of Mound Cemetery*, October 31, 2013, http://pioneerprologue.blogspot.com/2013/10/sally-dodge-cram-green-restless-spirit.html.

12. During this era, doctors needed specimens to teach their students and advance knowledge, but religious beliefs and superstition prevented most people from donating their body to science, hence the practice of grave robbing became common.

13. Harvey Wickes Felter, *History of the Eclectic Medical Institute, Cincinnati, Ohio 1845–1902* (Cincinnati, OH: Alumni Association of the Eclectic Medical Institute, 1902), 16–17.

14. These ideas were fueled by the bigoted notion that Native Americans and their ancestors were incapable of the complex thought required to create these structures. Spanish explorers, lost tribes of Israel and even the people of Atlantis were considered as the architects of the mounds.

15. Lynn Sturtevant, *Haunted Marietta* (Charleston, SC: The History Press, 2010), 74–75.

16. Summers, *History of Marietta*, 301–304.

17. Romain, *Shamans of the Lost World*.

18. R. Hall, "Ghosts, Water Barriers, Corn, and Sacred Enclosures in the Eastern Woodlands," *American Antiquity* 41, no. 3 (1976): 360–64.

19. Mason Winfield, "A Glint at the Mound," April 22, 2018, https://www.masonwinfield.com/a-glint-at-the-mound.

20. John Emsley, "Science: Graveyard Ghosts Are a Gas," *New Scientist*, June 18, 1993, https://www.newscientist.com/article/mg13818782-700-science-graveyard-ghosts-are-a-gas.

21. Ohio Exploration Society, "Mound Cemetery—Contribution," July 19, 2004, https://www.ohioexploration.com/paranormal/stories/story-moundcemetery.

22. Janette Quackenbush and Patrick Quackenbush, *Ohio Ghost Hunter Guide II: Haunted Hocking—A Ghost Hunter's Guide to the Hocking Hills and Beyond* (Athens, OH: 21 Crows Dusk to Dawn Publishing, 2011), 165–67.

23. Strutevant, *Haunted Marietta*, 74–75

24. Tiffany Royal, "What Ghosts Live in Your Room?," *The Post* (Athens, OH), October 26, 2000.

25. Craig Tremblay, *Guide to Ohio University Ghosts & Legends* (N.p.: Lulu Inc., 2007).

26. Brigette Mallon, "Greek Houseghosts," *The Post* (Athens, OH), October 26, 2010.

27. Lois Richtand, "The Ghost of Halloween Past," *The Post* (Athens, OH), October 25, 1979.

28. *Athens (OH) Messenger*, September 2, 1886.

29. *Athens (OH) Messenger*, December 1, 1854.

30. FamilySearch, "Mary Ann Roberts," Church of Jesus Christ of Latter-day Saints, genealogy submitted from MyTrees.com, 2022, https://www.familysearch.org/ark:/61903/2:2:Q49P-RBH.

31. *Athens (OH) Messenger*, November 3, 1881.

32. C.H. Harris, "District Tales of Long Ago," *Athens (OH) Sunday Messenger*, June 21, 1936.

33. Martha Hooke and Paul Danison, "Cemetery Mystery Lives," *The Post* (Athens, OH), November 10, 1970.

34. David Blumberg and Bruce Jorgenson, "Raising the Devil—Conant's Crusaders," *The Post* (Athens, OH), October 31, 1969.

35. Ibid.

36. Ibid.

37. Lois Richtand, "The Ghost of Halloween Past," *The Post* (Athens, OH), October 25, 1979.

38. Waymarking, "Haning Cemetery—Athens County, Ohio," November 16, 2011, https://www.waymarking.com/waymarks/WMCK9T_Haning_Cemetery_Athens_County_OH.

39. *Athens (OH) Messenger and Herald*, November 21, 1895.

40. Ancestry, "James K. Henry and Mary Angle," *Ohio, U.S., County Marriage Records, 1774–1993*, database online, Lehi, UT, Ancestry.com Operations Inc., 2016, https://www.ancestrylibrary.com/discoveryui-content/view/1341624:61378?tid=&pid=&queryId=9f648980a8b17a6975be7d1098d4cfd0&_phsrc=t08-268665&_phstart=successSource.

41. Ancestry, "James Kennedy Henry," listing with images, December 21, 2021, https://www.ancestry.com; Haunted Ohio image, originally posted on July 4, 2008, https://www.ancestrylibrary.com/mediaui-viewer/collection/1030/tree/26776649/person/5000058046/media/e8149a93-e433-4e9f-9da3-abfe79477b45?_phsrc=t081814021&usePUBJs=true.

42. Ibid.

43. Ancestry, "James K. Henry and Mary Angle."

44. *Newark (OH) Advocate*, December 29, 1971.

45. Ancestry, "Family Tree Listing," James Kennedy Henry, 1813–1849, https://www.ancestrylibrary.com/family-tree/person/tree/26776649/person/5000058046/facts?_phsrc=t081830130&_phstart=successSource.

46. *Daily Advocate* (Greenville, OH), December 5, 1928.

47. *Newark (OH) Advocate*, December 29, 1971.

48. *Athens (OH) Messenger*, "Church May Go to Court," March 7, 1973.

49. Eugene B. Willard, *A Standard History of the Hanging Rock Region of Ohio* (Chicago: Lewis Publishing Company, 1916), 391.

50. Find a Grave, "G.W. Elliot, Memorial ID 128139201," https://www.findagrave.com/memorial/128139201/g-w-elliott.

51. Ghosts and Ghouls, "Ohio's Haunted Salem Church Cemetery," 2022, https://ghostsnghouls.com/haunted-salem-church-cemetery.

52. Ibid.

53. Daniel Webster Williams, *A History of Jackson County, Ohio* (Jackson, OH, 1900), 184.

54. Ibid., 184–86.

55. Ibid.

56. Ibid.

57. Ghosts and Ghouls, "Ohio's Haunted Salem Church Cemetery."

58. Lora Schmidt Cahill and David L. Mowery, *Morgan's Raid Across Ohio: The Civil War Guidebook of the John Hunt Morgan Heritage Trail* (Columbus: Ohio Historical Society, 2014), 129.

59. *Athens (OH) Messenger*, "Church May Go to Court."

60. Ibid.

61. Ghosts and Ghouls, "Ohio's Haunted Salem Church Cemetery."

62. Ibid.

63. Henry Holcomb Bennett, *The County of Ross: A History of Ross County, Ohio*, vol. 2 (Madison, WI: Selwyn A. Brant, 1902), 286.

64. Ibid., 2:288.

65. Clyde Ford, "Is Halloween Dead?," *Chillicothe (OH) Gazette*, October 28, 1983.

66. *Chillicothe (OH) Gazette*, "The Property Appraised," October 14, 1896.

67. FamilySearch, "Ohio, County Death Records, 1840–2001," March 1, 2021, https://familysearch.org/ark:/61903/1:1:QVNS-6CDH, Elizabeth Eagleson, May 6, 1896, citing Death, South Union, Ross, Ohio, United States, source ID 52 11, county courthouses, Ohio, FHL microfilm 281,660.

68. Patti Cottrill, Julie Kleinhans and Clay Miller, "The Haunting Season," *Chillicothe (OH) Gazette*, September 27, 1991.

69. Find a Grave, "Elizabeth 'Lizzie' Beard Augustus," Memorial ID 26798907, https://www.findagrave.com/memorial/26798907/elizabeth-augustus.

70. Jan Angilella, "Total Disrespect at Union Township Cemetery," *Chillicothe (OH) Gazette*, April 27, 1987.

71. Armstrong Neighborhood Channel, "Exploring Local History—Lawrence County Museum," YouTube video, 31:00, December 12, 2016, https://youtu.be/Cj-mIhdcmU0.

72. *Ironton Tribune*, March 1, 2020.

73. Heath Harrison, "A Gorey Legacy: Author and Illustrator's Ashes Buried at Woodlawn in 2000," *Ironton Tribune*, August 10, 2019.

74. Ibid.

75. *Ironton Tribune*, July 17, 2018.

76. *Ironton Tribune*, May 26, 2021.

77. U.S. Federal Census, 1900, Ohio, Lawrence County, Mason, District 0071, Sheet 17.

78. Ohio Southern, "2020 Lawrence County Historical Society Ghost Walk," YouTube video, 1:09:44, October 24, 2020, https://youtu.be/o-3Ehrw35gE.

79. Briggs Lawrence County Public Library, "Wilson, Osa," 2022, https://www.briggslibrary.com/content/wilson-scott-and-osa.

80. Theresa Racer, "Ironton's Woodlawn Cemetery," Theresa's Haunted History of the Tri-State, May 31, 2011, http://theresashauntedhistoryofthetri-state.blogspot.com/2011/05/irontons-woodland-cemetery.html.

81. Theresa Moore, "Mausoleum Vandalized at Woodlawn Cemetery," *Ironton Tribune*, June 16, 2010.

82. Chris Woodyard, *Ghost Hunter's Guide to Haunted Ohio* (Dayton, OH: Kestrel Press, 2000), 179–80.

83. *Portsmouth (OH) Times*, July 12, 1933.

84. *East Liverpool (OH) Review*, July 5, 1933.

85. Ibid.

86. Racer, "Ironton's Woodlawn Cemetery."

87. Woodyard, *Ghost Hunter's Guide to Haunted Ohio*, 182.

88. Racer, "Ironton's Woodlawn Cemetery."

Part II

89. Louis H. Everts, *History of Clermont County, Ohio: With Illustrations and Biographical Sketches of Its Prominent Men and Pioneers of Southwestern Ohio* (Philadelphia, PA: J.B. Lippincott and Company, 1880), 324–25.
90. Ibid.
91. Ibid.
92. Ibid., 39.
93. Jim Shafer, *Historic Clermont County: An Illustrated History*, ed. Ron Hill and Patsy Shiveley (San Antonio, TX: Historical Publishing Network, 2010), 13.
94. H.H. Abels, "Sweet Lips," *Dayton Daily News*, July 8, 1951.
95. Everts, *History of Clermont County, Ohio*, 35.
96. Sabrina Schnarrenberg, "Smyrna Cemetery Restoration Project," *Clermont Sun*, May 18, 2017, https://www.clermontsun.com/2017/05/18/smyrna-cemetery-restoration-project.
97. *Dayton Daily News*, July 8, 1951.
98. Donald R. Johnson, "Clermont County Genealogical Society, Smyrna Cemetery," Rootsweb, August 3, 2007, https://sites.rootsweb.com/~ohclecgs/cemeteries/smyrna/index.html.
99. Interview with Mike Clephane, Franklin Township Historical Society, February 17, 2022.
100. Ohio Exploration Society, "Clermont County Hauntings & Legends," https://www.ohioexploration.com/paranormal/hauntings/clermontcounty.
101. There is an 1850 census listing for a twenty-eight-year-old woman named Agnes Cooper living in the area, but no other records exist to detail her life.
102. Rootsweb, "Smyrna Cemetery, Clermont County, Ohio," http://sites.rootsweb.com/~ohclecgs/cemeteries/smyrna/slides/cooper_agnes_not_sure.html.
103. Donald R. Johnson, "Smyrna Cemetery," Clermont County Genealogical Society, August 3, 2007, via Rootsweb, https://sites.rootsweb.com/~ohclecgs/cemeteries/smyrna/index.html.
104. In the April 28, 1885 edition of the *Ohio Xenia Gazette*, it was reported that a young woman in Middletown was literally frightened to death by a glimmering tombstone. An investigation revealed that it had only been reflecting a nearby light.
105. Ghosts of America, "Felicity, Ohio, Ghost Sightings," http://www.ghostsofamerica.com/4/Ohio_Felicity_ghost_sightings3.html.

106. John B. Jewett, "Fiddler's Green: A Story of the Miami Valley," *Cincinnati Commercial Gazette*, July 19, 1890.

107. Ibid.

108. Henry Howe, *Historical Collections of Ohio*, vol. 2 (Columbus, OH: Henry Howe and Son, 1891), 25.

109. Lewis Collins and Richard H. Collins, *Collins Historical Sketches of Kentucky. History of Kentucky*, vol. 2 (Covington, KY: Collins and Company, 1874), 435.

110. *Cincinnati Enquirer*, October 6, 1890.

111. Cecil Hale was a popular Cincinnati radio personality and professor at Mount St. Joseph University, near Darby-Lee Cemetery, and where he produced his 1963 play *The Legend of Fiddler's Green*.

112. White House Historical Association, "William Henry Harrison," https://www.whitehousehistory.org/bios/william-henry-harrison.

113. *Footprints* 35, no. 4, "Hidden Cemeteries Not Forgotten," (Fall 2012): 2, Delhi Historical Society, Cincinnati, Ohio.

114. Jeff Morris and Michael A. Morris, *Haunted Cincinnati and Southwest Ohio* (Charleston, SC: The History Press, 2009).

115. Ibid.

116. Julie Overton, "Clifton-Union Cemetery—Miami Township," Miami Township, 2021, https://miamitownship.net/clifton-union-cemetery.

117. *Springfield News-Sun*, November 12, 2004.

118. David A. Hustlar, "Lodrick Austin and the Driverless Stagecoach," *Echoes* 1, no. 10 (October 1962).

119. David J. Gerrick, *Ohio's Ghostly Greats* (Lorain, OH: Dayton Press, 1982).

120. William Albert Galloway, *The History of Glen Helen* (Columbus, OH: F.J. Heer Printing Company, 1932).

121. *Dayton Daily News*, August 28, 1983.

122. *(Dayton) Journal Herald*, June 20, 1977.

123. R.S. Dills, *History of Greene County, Together with Historic Notes on the Northwest and the State of Ohio* (Dayton, OH: Odell and Mayer, 1881), 676–77.

124. Ibid.; *Huron Reflector* (Norwalk, OH), September 4, 1849.

125. *Springfield (OH) News-Sun*, November 12, 2004.

126. *Cincinnati Commercial Tribune*, April 13, 1901.

127. *Hamilton (OH) Daily Republican News*, April 13, 1901.

128. *Cincinnati Enquirer*, April 18, 1901.

129. *Cincinnati Enquirer*, June 29, 1901.

130. *Cincinnati Commercial Tribune*, July 12, 1901.

131. *Cincinnati Enquirer*, April 18, 1901.

132. Karen Laven, *Cincinnati Ghosts* (Atglen, PA: Schiffer Publishing, 2008), 119–27.

133. *Cincinnati Enquirer*, October 24, 1938.

134. Christopher Magan, "Rose Hill Cemetery Sexton's Job Short on Ghosts," *Dayton Daily News*, November 2, 2006.

135. *Dayton Daily News*, November 2, 2006.

136. Founded by Dr. J.D. Commins in 1839, Glendale Cemetery, in Akron, is Ohio's first rural cemetery.

137. *Dayton Daily Empire*, July 1, 1859.

138. *Dayton Daily Journal*, August 17, 1860.

139. Joy Neighbors, "Devoted Pets and the Cemeteries They Inhabit: Part 2," A Grave Interest, May 6, 2011, https://agraveinterest.blogspot.com/search/label/Daniel%20LaDow?m=0.

140. John B. Kachuba, *Ghosthunting Ohio* (Cincinnati, OH: Emmis Books, 2004).

141. Donna Black-Sword, "Johnny and His Dog," House BlackSword, May 8, 2020, https://houseblacksword.com/tag/woodland-cemetery.

142. Andrew Henderson, "Woodland Cemetery," Forgotten Ohio, accessed via Internet Archive, https://web.archive.org/web/20021121042608/http://www.forgottenohio.com.

143. Kachuba, *Ghosthunting Ohio*.

144. David Weatherly, "Haunted Woodland Cemetery, Dayton, Ohio," Eerie Lights, August 15, 2019, https://eerielights.com/eerielightsblog/haunted-woodland-cemetery-dayton-ohio.

145. *Stark County (OH) Democrat*, May 31, 1877.

146. Dan Smith and Teri Casper, *Ghosts of Cincinnati: The Dark Side of the Queen City* (Charleston, SC: The History Press, 2009).

147. *Cincinnati Enquirer*, May 18, 1889.

148. Stella Perrin's mother, Melissa Elizabeth Riddle Banta, reflected on her loss in the poem "The Gruesome Rain."

149. This was likely because she had been buried in an airtight cast-iron casket. These were used at the time to not only slow decomposition but also prevent victims of infectious disease from contaminating the soil in which they were buried.

150. Ancestry, "Chas C. Brener," Year: 1880; Census Place: Cincinnati, Hamilton, Ohio; Roll: 1026; Page: 72C; Enumeration District: 151, https://www.ancestrylibrary.com/discoveryui-content/view/25794274:6742?tid=&pid=&queryId=67ff44294fb18f9d25b8832dd323184b&_phsrc=306-1514412&_phstart=successSource.

151. *Cincinnati Enquirer*, June 23, 1886.

152. *Cincinnati Enquirer*, March 21, 1896.

153. *Cincinnati Enquirer*, August 21, 1905.

154. *Cincinnati Enquirer*, September 14, 1905.

155. *Marion (OH) Daily Mirror*, May 23, 1908.

156. *Cincinnati Enquirer*, January 19, 1908.

157. *Cincinnati Enquirer*, January 18, 1908.

158. *Cincinnati Enquirer*, April 30, 1908.

159. *Cincinnati Enquirer*, July 12, 1908.

160. *Cincinnati Enquirer*, May 2, 1904.

161. *Cincinnati Enquirer*, May 3, 1904.

162. Ibid.

163. *Washington Times*, November 13, 1904.

164. *Cincinnati Enquirer*, November 5, 1904.

165. *Cincinnati Enquirer*, January 2, 1910.

166. *Cincinnati Enquirer*, October 26, 1910.

167. *Marion (OH) Daily Mirror*, October 26, 1910.

168. *Tacoma Times*, November 8, 1910.

Part III

169. Isaac Smucker, *Centennial History of Licking County, Ohio* (Newark, OH: Clark and Underwood, 1876), 169.

170. Sue (username), "RE: 1830s Johnstown," Ancestry Message Boards, posted June 11, 2002, https://www.ancestrylibrary.com/boards/localities.northam.usa.states.ohio.counties.licking/1976?viewType=FLAT_VIEW.

171. Christine (username), "RE: Followup to Sarah for Sue," Ancestry Message Boards, posted June 13, 2002, https://www.ancestrylibrary.com/boards/localities.northam.usa.states.ohio.counties.licking/1976?viewType=FLAT_VIEW&page=1.

172. Nola Miles Rogers (username), "RE: 1830s Johnstown," Ancestry Message Boards, posted June 6, 2002, https://www.ancestrylibrary.com/boards/localities.northam.usa.states.ohio.counties.licking/1976?viewType=FLAT_VIEW&page=1.

173. There is a similar legend relating to this poem at the grave of Annabelle Davis in Ridgeway Cemetery, in Hardin County.

174. Shannon (username), "Johnstown Ohio Ghost Sightings—PAGE 2," Ghosts of America, http://www.ghostsofamerica.com/4/Ohio_Johnstown_ghost_sightings2.html.

175. James Miller, "Faith Survives Fire," *Newark (OH) Advocate*, November 2, 1999.

176. William Little, *The History of Weare, New Hampshire, 1735–1888* (Lowell, MA: S.W. Huse & Company, 1888), 417.

177. Salem Witch Trials Documentary Archive and Transcription Project, "SWP No. 47: Martha Emerson," https://salem.lib.virginia.edu/n47. html.

178. Rebecca Beatrice Brooks, "Roger Toothaker and Family: Witches or Witch Killers?," *History of Massachusetts Blog*, January 30, 2012, https://historyofmassachusetts.org/the-toothaker-family-witches-or-witch-killers.

179. Legends of America, "Witches of Massachusetts—T," https://www.legendsofamerica.com/ma-witches-t.

180. Samuel Parks, *Notes of the Early History of Union Township: Licking County, Ohio* (Terre Haute, IN: O.J. Smith and Company, 1870).

181. *Columbus (OH) Sunday Dispatch*, November 22, 1903.

182. Ibid.

183. Ibid.

184. Parks, *Notes of the Early History of Union Township*.

185. Ibid.

186. *Columbus (OH) Evening Dispatch*, April 5, 1904.

187. Parks, *Notes of the Early History of Union Township*.

188. *Columbus (OH) Sunday Dispatch*, November 22, 1903.

189. C.M.U. Wiseman, *Pioneer Period and Pioneer People of Fairfield County, Ohio* (Columbus, OH: Heer Printing Company, 1901).

190. *Columbus (OH) Sunday Dispatch*, November 22, 1903.

191. Ibid.

192. Ibid.

193. Ohio History Connection, "American Civil War," https://ohiohistorycentral.org/w/American_Civil_War.

194. My Civil War, "Camp Chase Prisoner of War Camp," https://www.mycivilwar.com/pow/oh-camp-chase.html.

195. Lois Neff, "History of Camp Chase," Hilltop Historical Society, https://hilltopusa.tripod.com/id16.html.

196. Ibid.

197. National Park Service, U.S. Department of the Interior, "Camp Chase Confederate Cemetery, Columbus, Ohio," https://www.nps.gov/nr/travel/national_cemeteries/ohio/camp_chase_confederate_cemetery.html.

198. Dennis Ranney, Camp Chase Confederate Cemetery, 2020, https://www.campchase.us.

199. Interview with an anonymous source, October 10, 2016.

200. *Cleveland Plain Dealer*, February 8, 1887.

201. Virginia Lamkin, "The Gray Lady of Camp Chase," Seeks Ghosts, September 20, 2015 https://seeksghosts.blogspot.com/2015/09/the-gray-lady-of-camp-chase.html.

202. David Roth, ed., "Guide to Haunted Places of the Civil War," *Blue & Gray* (1996).

203. Ibid.

204. Bob Waldron, "The Veiled Lady of Camp Chase," *Columbus (OH) Dispatch*, December 24, 1961.

205. Ancestry, "Joseph M. Briggs and Louisanna A. Ransburgh," *Ohio, U.S., County Marriage Records, 1774–1993*, database online, Lehi, UT, Ancestry.com Operations Inc., 2016.

206. Franklin County Genealogical Society, *Franklin County, Ohio Cemeteries*, vol. 10, *Jackson & Pleasant Townships* (Columbus, OH: self-published, 1988).

207. Experiences with the Supernatural (COMPSTD235OH), "Wollyburger Cemetery," Ohio State University, https://u.osu.edu/supernaturalfolkloreproject2020/wollyburger-cemetery.

208. James A. Willis, *Central Ohio Legends & Lore* (Charleston, SC: The History Press, 2017), 147.

209. *A Centennial Biographical History of the City of Columbus, and Franklin County, Ohio* (Chicago: Lewis Publishing Company, 1901), 366–68; James F. Hale, "Pleasant Township," Southwest Franklin County Historical Society, 2020, http://grovecityohhistory.org/pleasant-township.

210. *Columbus (OH) Evening Dispatch*, August 25, 1877.

211. *Columbus (OH) Dispatch*, August 6, 1898.

212. *Columbus (OH) Evening Dispatch*, March 26, 1957.

213. James Breiner and Gary Kiefer, "Columbus Man Slain, Corpse Found Floating in Pond," *Columbus (OH) Dispatch*, November 25, 1979.

214. Richard Bloom, "Kidnapping Victim Kills Abductor," *Columbus (OH) Dispatch*, October 24, 1981.

215. Richard Bloom, "Kidnapper Worked for Man Who Killed Him," *Columbus (OH) Dispatch*, October 25, 1981.

216. Donald M. Schlegel, *The Columbus City Graveyards* (Columbus, OH: Columbus History Service, 1985), 6.

217. William T. Martin, *History of Franklin County: A Collection of Reminiscence of the Early Settlement of the County; With Biographical Sketches and a Complete History of the County to the Present Time* (Columbus, OH: Follett, Foster, & Company, 1858), 394.

218. *The Medium & Daybreak: A Weekly Journal Devoted to the History, Phenomena, Philosophy and Teachings of Spiritualism*, vol. 14 (London: J. Burns Progressive Library and Spiritual Institution, 1883), 244.

219. *Columbus (OH) Sunday Dispatch*, July 24, 1960.

220. Grandview Heights/Marble Cliff Historical Society, "Hayden Mausoleum—Greenlawn," https://www.ghmchs.org/hayden-mausoleum-greenlawn.

221. FamilySearch, "Ohio, County Death Records, 1840–2001," database with images, March 1, 2021, https://familysearch.org/ark:/61903/1:1:F6JK-64X, Eva M Wagner, September 1880, citing Death, Columbus, Franklin, Ohio, United States, source ID v 1 p 169, county courthouses, Ohio; FHL microfilm 285,206.

222. *Columbus (OH) Evening Dispatch*, September 3, 1833.

223. Ibid.

Part IV

224. Thomas Mikesell, *The County of Fulton, a History of Fulton County, Ohio, from the Earliest Days, with Special Chapters on Various Subjects, Including Each of the Different Townships; Also a Biographical Department* (Madison, WI: Northwestern Historical Association, 1905).

225. Ibid.

226. Bob Downing, "Ohio Nature Preserve Showcases Giant Trees, Woodland," *Dayton Daily News*, February 29, 2004.

227. Another commonly made claim is that a black tombstone at the center of the cemetery is always warm to the touch. There is nothing supernatural about that, however, as it is simple science that a dark color absorbs more heat. And for what it's worth, there is also a distinct possibility that the lights seen in the cemetery are swamp gas. The surrounding area is, after all, a swamp.

228. *Northwestern Republican* (Wauseon, OH), August 14, 1873; January 20, 1876.

229. TJ Riviere, "Haunting of Gollwoods," Geneaology, September 14, 2004, https://www.genealogy.com/forum/regional/states/topics/oh/fulton/193.

230. Mike Mignin and Haunted Toledo, "Goll Woods State Nature Preserve," via Facebook, December 20, 2016, https://www.facebook.com/HauntedToledo/photos/goll-woods-state-nature-preservearchbold-ohioohio-folklore-is-full-of-legends-wh/1295228757211105.

231. Toledo Ohio Ghost Hunters Society, "Goll Woods," May 30, 2009, https://toghs.org/2009/05/30/golls-woods.

232. Writer's Program (Ohio), *Bryan and Williams County* (Gallipolis, OH: Downtain Printing Company, 1941), 81–82.

233. Ibid., 77–78.

234. Charles B. Norton, *The Transactions of the American Medical Association* (New York: Baker, Godwin, & Company, Printers, 1854), 394.

235. Marguerite Calvin, *People and Places: Putnam County, Ohio, 1800–1900* (Defiance, OH: Hubbard, 1981), 80.

236. D.L. Spangler, "'August 1852' on Graves Tells Tragedy of Cholera that Ravaged Gilboa Then," *Findlay Morning Republican*, August 31, 1933.

237. Norton, *Transactions of the American Medical Association*, 394.

238. D.L. Spangler, "Fourteen Persons Died in Cholera Epidemic at Gilboa 100 Years Ago," *Findlay Republican Courier*, August 12, 1952.

239. Calvin, *People and Places*, 112.

240. Ibid., 82.

241. *Putnam County, Ohio, Cemeteries, Blanchard Township*, vol. 7 (Ottawa, OH: Putnam County Genealogical Society, 1993).

242. Melissa Davies, interview with Nancy Klein, via *Ohio Folklore: Gilboa's Haunted Cholera Cemetery*, podcast audio, April 18, 2021, https://www.buzzsprout.com/236393/8356776-gilboa-s-haunted-cholera-cemetery.

243. Ibid.

244. *Defiance Crescent News*, August 26, 1926.

245. Davies, interview with Klein.

246. Ashleigh Klinger. "The Legend of the Hatchet Man," Peak of Ohio, October 21, 2011, https://www.peakofohio.com/news/details.cfm?id=10293.

247. *Baltimore Sun*, December 27, 1843.

248. Joshua Antrim, *The History of Champaign and Logan Counties, From Their First Settlements* (Bellefontaine, OH: Press Printing Company, 1872), 79–126.

249. Ibid.

250. Antrim, *History of Champaign and Logan Counties*, 83–84.

251. Ibid.

252. Ibid.

253. Ibid.

254. Ibid., 100.

255. *Baltimore Sun*, May 1, 1843.

256. *Brooklyn (NY) Evening Star*, January 16, 1844.

257. *Baltimore Sun*, December 27, 1843.

258. Gayleen Gindy, *Sylvania, Lucas County, Ohio: From Footpaths to Expressways and Beyond*, vol. 5 (Bloomington, IN: Authorhouse, 2015).

259. Find a Grave. "Nettie Cameson Hallis," Memorial ID 194533740, https://www.findagrave.com/memorial/194533740/nettie-hollis.

260. After being found guilty of murdering and dismembering his wife, Olive, in 1857, Return Ward confessed to the 1850 murder of Planktown, Ohio shopkeeper Noah Hall, as well as the killing of a traveling salesman by the name of Lovejoy about one year later. While Return Ward's callous indifference toward human life qualifies him as a monstrous being, his murders didn't follow a pattern, as is characteristic of serial killers. Also, he was not the first Ohioan to take the lives of multiple people. Even though he didn't admit to the crime of poisoning his children, Andrew Hellman likely took the lives of three members of his family at Huntsville in 1839. There was also Samuel Bushong, who, according to Albert Adams Graham's *The History of Richland County, Ohio*, used an axe to murder his wife and two teenage daughters in October 1840. He attempted to kill his two sons as well, although they managed to wrestle the weapon away from their father and detain him until a marshal could be summoned. After a very short trial, Bushong was found not guilty by reason of insanity. Upon his release, he fled the state.

261. Paula Miner, "Ghosts Still Haunt Area Graveyards," *Toledo (OH) Blade*, October 31, 1970.

262. Minerva Merrymaker, "The Secrets of the Cemeteries," Haunted Sylvania, 2013, https://www.hauntedsylvania.com/sylvaniacemeteries.

263. Find a Grave, "Eliza Chamberlain Bidwell," Memorial ID 39740896, https://www.findagrave.com/memorial/39740896/eliza-bidwell.

264. FamilySearch, Bosworth W. Trombly and Eliza Bidwell, 1888, "Ohio, County Marriages, 1789–2016," database with images, September 29, 2021, https://www.familysearch.org/ark:/61903/1:1:X8H3-TZG.

265. Gayleen Gindy, "Sylvania—Then and Now," *Sylvania Advantage*, September 1, 2020, 4A, https://pubhtml5.com/rfxc/vxpe.

266. Find a Grave, "Eliza Chamberlain Bidwell."

267. Gindy, "Sylvania—Then and Now."

268. Facebook, "Haunted Toledo," https://www.facebook.com/Haunted Toledo/posts/ravine-cemeterysylvania-ohioone-of-the-most-popular-and-enduring-legends-in-luca/1284478451619469.

269. Nevin Otto Winter, *A History of Northwest Ohio: A Narrative Account of Its Historical Progress and Development from Its First European Exploration of the Maumee and Sandusky Valleys and the Adjacent Shores of Lake Erie, down to the Present Time*, vol. 1 (Chicago: Lewis Publishing Company, 1917), 273.

270. Wendy Koile, *Disasters of Ohio's Lake Erie Islands* (Charleston, SC: The History Press, 2015), 26.

271. Winter, *History of Northwest Ohio*.

272. Ibid.

273. *Cleveland Plain Dealer*, November 8, 1964.

274. *Cleveland Plain Dealer*, February 8, 1887.

275. J.R. Johnson, "The Ghosts of the Confederacy," *Cleveland Plain Dealer*, April 11, 1911.

276. Haunted Places, "Johnson's Island Confederate Cemetery," https://www.hauntedplaces.org/item/johnsons-island-confederate-cemetery.

277. Ashley Herzog, "The Time I Caught a Ghost on Camera," VocalMedia, https://vocal.media/horror/the-time-i-caught-a-ghost-on-camera.

278. Donald L. Barlett, "LHS Is Sick; Law Changes Prescribed," *Cleveland Plain Dealer*, June 6, 1965.

279. Donald L. Barlett, "Teen-Agers in Criminal Dump at Lima," *Cleveland Plain Dealer*, May 23, 1965.

280. *Lima (OH) News*, March 8, 1928.

281. *Newark (OH) Advocate*, March 8, 1928.

282. *Daily News Tribune (Greenville, OH)*, March 8, 1928.

283. *Cleveland Plain Dealer*, "50 Exclusive Stories Showed Lima Horror," August 7, 1971.

284. *Cincinnati Post*, "Charges Detailed Against Group Accused in State Hospital Probe," November 24, 1971.

285. Richard C. Widman, "Lima Witness Found Healthy for Job in '71," *Cleveland Plain Dealer*, December 31, 1971.

286. Robert H. Snyder, "Lima Trial Deal Was Hatched in Wee Hours Saturday," *Cleveland Plain Dealer*, July 12, 1972.

287. *Cleveland Plain Dealer*, "Reinstated Lima Attendant Charged with Beating Kin," August 11, 1972.

288. Jerry M. Flint, "31 Ex-Employees at Ohio Hospital Appear in Court," *New York Times*, November 27, 1971.

289. *Dover (OH) Daily Reporter*, March 16, 1962.

290. Edward P. Whelan and Richard C. Widman, "Lima's Inmates Exist Amid Fear, Brutality," *Cleveland Plain Dealer*, May 14, 1971.

291. *Bath Township, Allen County, Ohio Cemeteries* (Lima, OH: Allen County Genealogical Society, 1998), 55.

292. Edward P. Whelan and Richard C. Widman, "Lima Hospital Birth Ordeal Described by Ex-Attendant," *Cleveland Plain Dealer*, June 17, 1971.

293. eksohorg (username), City-Data.com. "Lima State Hospital—Lima, Ohio." posted March 20, 2010, https://www.city-data.com/forum/ohio/58882-lima-state-hospital-lima-ohio-5.html.

294. Mark Sebastian Jordan, *The Ceely Rose Murders at Malabar Farm* (Charleston, SC: The History Press, 2021), 18.

295. Kat Klockow, "In Search of Ghosts at Malabar Farm," Katklockow, June 16, 2014, http://www.katklockow.com/?p=241.

296. Jordan, *Ceely Rose Murders*.

297. Ibid.

298. Kenny Libben, "Triple Murder in Pleasant Valley Resonates from 1896," *Ashland Source*, October 6, 2019, https://www.ashlandsource.com/history/triple-murder-in-pleasant-valley-resonates-from-1896/article_67a3f414-cf1d-11e9-9e89-e7abbb4b8951.html.

299. *Butler (OH) Enterprise*, September 17, 1896.

300. *Cleveland Plain Dealer*, "Celia Rose Is a Moral Pervert," October 6, 1896.

301. FamilySearch, "Ohio Deaths, 1908–1953," database with images, May 21, 2014, https://www.familysearch.org/ark:/61903/3:1:S3HT-67MQ-5WL?i=2091&cc=1307272&personaUrl=%2Fark%3A%2F61903%2F1%3A1%3AX6X1-8Y6.

302. Greg Hoersten, "Murder in 1896," *Lima (OH) News*, October 30, 2013.

303. Steve Stephens, "Richland County Rich in Sites of Ghostly Lore," *Columbus (OH) Dispatch*, October 17, 2021.

304. Jordan, *Ceely Rose Murders*.

305. Janette Quackenbush, *Ohio Ghost Hunters Guide V: Haunted Hocking* (Athens, OH: 21 Crows Dusk to Dawn Publishing, 2013), 16.

306. Ohio Haunt and Paranormal, "#91 Return to Lima State Hospital Cemetery," YouTube video, 6 minutes, posted April 17, 2018, https://youtu.be/BbRJIC44dvw.

Part V

307. In 1972, Dr. Orrin Shane used the burial as a field school for his students at Kent State University. At that time, they removed the sheet of tar paper that George Towner has placed over the grave in 1932.

308. Joan Madden, "Portage County Hauntings and Legends: Towner's Woods Park," Ohio Exploration Society, https://www.ohioexploration.com/paranormal/hauntings/portagecounty.

309. *Akron Beacon Journal*, October 25, 1983.

310. *(East Liverpool) Evening Review*, July 31, 1931.

311. Chloe Bragg, "Towner Mound: Creating Content and Sparking Curiosity for the Portage County Parks," thesis, Kent State University, 2015, http://rave.ohiolink.edu/etdc/view?acc_num=ksuhonors1430692663.

312. *Akron Beacon Journal*, July 18, 1932.

313. Bragg, "Towner Mound."

314. *Akron Beacon Journal*, July 10, 1933.

315. Munroe Falls Paranormal Society, "Towner's Woods Flute Sound," YouTube video, 1:36, October 25, 2009, https://www.youtube.com/watch?v=DwTC93B0uKw.

316. Dead Ohio, "Towner's Woods," last modified November 3, 2015, via the Wayback Machine, http://deadohio.com/townerswoods.

317. Ancestry, "Anne Maria Lutzen," *Ohio, U.S., County Marriage Records, 1774–1993*, database online, Lehi, UT, Ancestry.com Operations Inc., 2016.

318. Joanna Ross, *Coshocton Tribune*, November 11, 1967.

319. N.N. Hill, *History of Coshocton County, Ohio: Its Past and Present, 1740–1881* (Newark, OH: A.A. Graham and Company, 1881), 270–71.

320. Susan Nolan, "Mary Stockum Rest in Peace Coshocton, Ohio Urban Legend," YouTube video, 9:16, January 8, 2020, https://youtu.be/f7c4AUe7aG0.

321. Karen Gray, "Adam Burwell Letter," *Rose Township Carroll County, Ohio* (Ohio: Carroll County Historical Society, 2008).

322. Velma Griffin, "Is Morges Rectory Haunted?," *Dover Times Reporter*, July 13, 1973.

323. Ibid.

324. Karen Gray, "St. Mary's Catholic Church," *Rose Township Carroll County, Ohio* (Ohio: Carroll County Historical Society, 2008).

325. Moina W. Large, *History of Ashtabula County*, vol. 1 (Topeka, IN: Historical Publishing Company, 1924), 189.

326. *Cleveland Plain Dealer*, "The Railway Wreck," January 2, 1877.

327. Stephen D. Peet, *The Ashtabula Disaster* (Chicago: J.S. Goodman and Louis Lloyd & Company, 1877), 66.

328. *Cleveland Plain Dealer*, "Railway Wreck."

329. *Cleveland Plain Dealer*, "The Blood-Curdling Casualty," December 30, 1876.

330. *Cleveland Plain Dealer*, "Relics from the Wreck," January 5, 1877.

331. *Cleveland Plain Dealer*, December 23, 1979.

332. Darrell E. Hamilton, "Almost the Perfect Disaster," in *Bliss and Tragedy: The Ashtabula Railway Bridge Accident of 1876 and the Loss of P.P. Bliss*, ed. Thomas E. Corts (Birmingham, AL: Samford University Press, 2003), 6.

333. *Cincinnati Enquirer*, January 20, 1877.

334. *Cleveland Plain Dealer*, January 20, 1877.

335. Amasa Stone refused to accept that his bridge design was flawed despite the findings of several investigations that confirmed this to be the case. He committed suicide seven years after the disaster and Collins's death.

336. Engineering Tragedy, "Charles Collins: The Ashtabula Train Disaster," 2012, Beacon Productions LLC, https://www.engineeringtragedy.com/charles-collins.

337. JackMc, "Ghosts of the Ashtabula River Bridge Disaster," Mid-Western Ghosts and Hauntings, October 24, 2011, http://midwesternghostsandhauntings.blogspot.com/2011/10/ghosts-of-ashtabula-river-bridge.html.

338. Margie Trax, "Former Cemetery Worker Has Seen Ghosts," *Ashtabula Star Beacon*, October 31, 2004.

339. NorthCoastParanorm, "Chestnut Grove Cemetery 'Help Me,'" YouTube video, 31 seconds, February 7, 2011, https://youtu.be/H5ZBb__5nMQ.

340. *Cleveland Plain Dealer*, May 19, 1890.

341. Urns containing the ashes of the Garfields' daughter, Mary "Mollie" Garfield Stanley-Brown, and her husband, Joseph Stanley-Brown, are also interred here.

342. Cleveland, "Cleveland Ghost Stories—A Bullet for a Ghost: Lakeview Cemetery," https://www.cleveland.com/haunted/blog/2008/10/cleveland_ghost_stories_a_bull.html.

343. National Park Service, U.S. Department of Interior, "Eliza Ballou Garfield," July 31, 2020, https://www.nps.gov/people/eliza-ballou-garfield.htm.

344. James A. Garfield National Historic Site, "James A. Garfield Dabbled in the Occult," October 31, 2020, via Facebook, https://www.facebook.com/GarfieldNPS/posts/3354701184584437.

345. A. Leah Underhill, *The Missing Link in Modern Spiritualism* (New York: Trow's Printing and Bookbinding Company, 1885).

346. Joel Martin and William J. Blimes, *The Haunting of the Presidents: A Paranormal History of the U.S. Presidency* (New York: New American Library, Penguin Putnam, 2003).

347. Ibid.

348. John D. Ehrhardt Jr. and J. Patrick O'Leary, "Yes, I Shot the President, but His Physicians Killed Him: The Assassination of President James A. Garfield," American College of Surgeons, 2017, https://www.facs.org/-/media/files/archives/shg-poster/2017/03_james_garfield.ashx.

349. Lisa Bramen, "Salisbury Steak: Civil War Health Food," *Smithsonian Magazine* (June 22, 2011), https://www.smithsonianmag.com/arts-culture/salisbury-steak-civil-war-health-food-18584973.

350. James Henry Salisbury, *The Relation and Alimentation of Disease* (New York: J.H. Vail and Company, 1888).

351. Bramen, "Salisbury Steak."

352. U.S. Congressional serial set, vol. 1375 (Washington, D.C.: Government Printing Office, 1869).

353. Drew Rolik, "Encyclopedia of Cleveland History," Wholesale Grocers, 2021, Case Western Reserve University, https://case.edu/ech/articles/w/wholesale-grocers.

354. Jessie Claire Glasier, *Cleveland Plain Dealer*, December 9, 1906.

355. Michelle Belanger, *Ghostly Experiences: Encounters with the Otherworldly* (Woodbury, MN: Llewellyn Publications, 2009).

356. Glasier, *Cleveland Plain Dealer*, December 9, 1906.

ABOUT THE AUTHOR

E.R. Cutright is the founder of Columbus Ghost Tours in Columbus, Ohio, where he has been sharing tales of history, mystery and legend since 2012.

Visit us at
www.historypress.com
···